JANE EYRE

Charlotte Bronte

AUTHORED by Teddy Wayne
UPDATED AND REVISED by Caitlin Vincent

COVER DESIGN by Table XI Partners LLC
COVER PHOTO by Olivia Verma and © 2005 GradeSaver, LLC

BOOK DESIGN by Table XI Partners LLC

Published by GradeSaver LLC, www.gradesaver.com

First published in the United States of America by GradeSaver LLC. 2009

ISBN 978-1-60259-169-1

Printed in the United States of America

For other products and additional information please visit http://www.gradesaver.com

Table of Contents

Biography of Bronte, Charlotte (1816-1855)....1

About Jane Eyre....5

Character List....7

Major Themes....15

Glossary of Terms....19

Short Summary....35

Quotes and Analysis....39

Summary and Analysis of Volume I, Chapters 1-5....45

Summary and Analysis of Volume I, Chapters 6-10....51

Summary and Analysis of Volume I, Chapters 11-15....55

Summary and Analysis of Volume II, Chapters 1-5....61

Summary and Analysis of Volume II, Chapters 6-11....67

Summary and Analysis of Volume III, Chapters 1-6....75

Summary and Analysis of Volume III, Chapters 7-12....81

Suggested Essay Questions....87

The Madwoman in the Attic: Angel or Monster?....91

Author of ClassicNote and Sources....93

Essay: Women in Literature: Examining Oppression Versus Independence in Henry V and Jane Eyre....95

Essay: Jane Eyre: The Independent and Successful Woman Of the Nineteenth Century....99

Quiz 1....103

Table of Contents

Quiz 1 Answer Key..109

Quiz 2..111

Quiz 2 Answer Key..117

Quiz 3..119

Quiz 3 Answer Key..125

Quiz 4..127

Quiz 4 Answer Key..133

Biography of Bronte, Charlotte (1816-1855)

Charlotte Brontë was the third child of the Reverend Patrick Brontë and Maria Branwell. Born in 1816, Charlotte was soon followed by her brother Patrick Branwell in 1817, her sister Emily in 1818, and her sister Ann in 1820. The four siblings had an extremely close relationship, and their childhood collaboration would lead to a creative spirit unexpected from the children of an Anglican clergyman. In 1821, the family moved to Haworth in Yorkshire, where the Reverend had been appointed Perpetual Curate. Maria Branwell died of cancer in 1821, leaving five daughters and one son in the care of their somewhat severe father.

In 1824, Reverend Brontë had his four eldest daughters sent to study at the Clergy Daughter's School in Cowan Bridge. Conditions at the school were poor, and fever constantly broke out at the school. Throughout her life, Charlotte would attribute the school's poor conditions to the deaths of her sisters Maria and Elizabeth, both of whom succumbed to tuberculosis. After the death of their sisters, Charlotte, Emily, and Anne were withdrawn from the school and brought home, and the children's aunt, Elizabeth Branwell, became their new instructor.

Though the remaining children were deeply affected by the death of their two sisters, they filled their spare time with imaginative fantasies and fictitious worlds. For example, after their father gave Patrick Branwell a box of toy soldiers in 1826, the children were inspired to invent and write sagas about imaginary worlds called Angria and Gondal. Considering the bleak surroundings of the Yorkshire countryside, it is not surprising that the Bronte children began to explore their powers of imagination at an early age.

In 1831, Charlotte was sent to study at the Roe Head School, an institution headed by Mrs. Wooler and containing seven to ten additional students. Because of her father's declining health, it was particularly important for Charlotte to have enough of an education to be able to be economically independent. Charlotte's time at the Roe Head School was difficult: her Irish accent, uneven education, and quaint manner of dressing set her apart from the other pupils at the school, and she suffered from extreme homesickness. However, Mrs. Wooler was an encouraging teacher and helped Charlotte to overcome the limits of her previous education. Charlotte eventually earned several awards for outstanding scholarship, and, in 1832, was offered a position as a teacher at the school.

Charlotte declined the offer to teach at the Roe Head School in order to return home and instruct her sisters, over whom she now had educational advantages. The majority of Charlotte's time was spent studying with her sisters, teaching Sunday school classes, exploring the moors, and writing short fictional works. She also corresponded frequently with Ellen Nussey and Mary Taylor, both of whom she had met at the Roe Head school. In 1835, Charlotte returned to Mrs. Wooler's school to teach while her sister Emily accompanied her as a pupil. Emily soon left the school because of homesickness but was replaced by her sister Ann.

Three years later, Charlotte left the Roe Head School in order to assume a position as a governess to the Sidgewick family. Leaving her post after only three months, Charlotte returned to Haworth. In 1841, she took a post as governess to the White family but, again, left after only a few months. In 1842, Charlotte and Emily traveled to Brussels in order to complete their education at a pensionnat run by the schoolmaster Constantin Hegin and his wife -- and exchanged English and music lessons for board and tuition. After a brief trip back to Haworth, Charlotte returned alone to Brussels and became emotionally attached to Hegin. When Charlotte's love was not reciprocated, she became overwhelmed with depression and returned to Haworth in 1844.

Upon Charlotte's return, she and Emily realized their dream of opening a school in Haworth. Unfortunately, the school was a complete failure: the advertisements for the school did not result in a single public response. With the failure of the school, Charlotte and her sisters were free to focus on their literary careers. Having discovered some of Emily's poems during the previous year, Charlotte decided to publish selected poems of all three sisters; in 1846, a collection of their poems was published under the pseudonyms of Currer, Ellis, and Acton Bell. Charlotte's first novel, "The Professor," was also written during this time, though it was initially rejected for publication and was met with very little enthusiasm. However, Charlotte's second novel, "Jane Eyre," was published the following year and was a resounding success. The same year also saw the publication of Emily's novel "Wuthering Heights" and Ann's "Agnes Grey."

In 1848, Charlotte visited her publisher in London and revealed the true identity of the "Bells." However, her happiness at their literary success was soon marred by the death of her brother, Patrick, followed shortly by the deaths of both Emily and Ann. Charlotte coped with her loss by spending time within the literary circles of London, among such making figures such as William James Thackeray, and striving to edit her sisters' works. At this point, Charlotte began to suffer from health problems of her own.

In 1852, the Reverend Arthur Bell Nicholls, the curate of Haworth since 1845, proposed marriage to Charlotte. Unfortunately, Charlotte's father was violently opposed to the match, and Charlotte refused to accept the proposal. According to many accounts, Charlotte was not in love with the Reverend Nicholls and thus, was not overly heartbroken at her father's opposition. In the midst of this disappointed courtship, Charlotte worked on her next novel, "Villette," which was published in 1853. The following year, the Reverend Brontë's opposition to the Reverend Nicholls faded, and the Reverend Nicholls renewed his proposal to Charlotte. Despite her seeming apathy towards him, Charlotte married him in 1854. Shortly after becoming pregnant, she was diagnosed with pneumonia and died of the disease in 1855. She was only thirty-nine years old.

Some biographers claim that Charlotte Brontë actually starved herself to death because of her dislike of her husband. Others argue that her death was merely a subconscious effort to relieve herself of the depression that had plagued her entire life. Charlotte's personal life was ultimately an unhappy one, and, according to her contemporary biographer Elizabeth Gaskell, Charlotte never harbored any hope for the future. The settings and themes of her novels and poems demonstrate this sense of hopelessness and also highlight her belief that God had appointed some people for sorrow and some people for happiness. Although "Jane Eyre" can be read as a happy novel, the isolated mentality of the heroine and the difficult circumstances of her upbringing clearly reflect Charlotte's own perception of the world.

About Jane Eyre

Published to widespread success in 1847 under the androgynous pseudonym of "Currer Bell," the novel "Jane Eyre" catapulted 31-year-old Charlotte Brontë into the upper echelon of Victorian writers. With the novel's success, Brontë was able to reveal her true identity to her publisher, and it soon became widely known that the author of the popular novel was a woman. This revelation allowed "Jane Eyre" to achieve an additional level of interest in contemporary society by forcing the public to redefine sexist notions of female authorship. Although the text presumably relates events from the first decade of the 19th century, contemporary Victorians, particularly women, identified with Brontë's critique of Victorian class and gender mores. In particular, Brontë's commentary on the difficult position of a governess during the time period was one with which many woman could relate and empathize.

Written as a first-person narrative, the novel follows the plain but intelligent Jane Eyre in her development as an individual from her traumatic childhood. Brontë describes five specific stages of Jane's growth over the course of the novel: first, her childhood among oppressive relatives; second, her time as a student at Lowood School; third, her months as a governess at Thornfield Manor; fourth, her time with her cousins at Marsh's End; and finally, her return to Thornfield Manor and marriage to Mr. Rochester. As a classic example of the Germanic Bildungsroman, or novel of formation, the text demonstrates Jane's attempts to define her identity against forces of opposition in each of these five stages.

Bronte also employs many elements of the Gothic novel, another classic literary tool from the period, in order to provide a more tragic bent to Jane's struggles. Mr. Rochester's characterization as a stereotypical Byronic hero, the ominously gothic nature of Thornfield Manor, Jane's unrequited love for Mr. Rochester, and the concept of the Madwoman in the Attic--each of these aspects of the novel relate directly to understandings of the Gothic tradition.

Many aspects of the novel are modeled on Brontë's own life. She wrote of the novel, "I will show you a heroine as plain and as small as myself," and, indeed, the characterization of the protagonist as unattractive was largely unheard of in Victorian literature. Like Jane, Bronte was forced to rely on her intellect in order to achieve economic independence and worked a governess with several different families. She attended the harsh evangelical Cowan Bridge School, on which she modeled Lowood. Moreover, the death of Helen Burns at Lowood is a clear reference to the deaths of Brontë's two sisters during their time at the Cowan Bridge School. John Reed's descent into gambling and alcoholism also parallels the behavior of Brontë's beloved brother, Patrick Branwell, who took to opium and alcohol and died the year after "Jane Eyre" was published.

The tragic and subdued tone of the novel also speaks to Brontë's personal experiences in a more general way. With the death of her mother and two elder sisters during her childhood, Brontë was forced to cope with a strict and severe father and grow up on the desolate moors of Yorkshire (which appear in all their bleakness in Emily Brontë's novel "Wuthering Heights"). The deaths of her three remaining siblings came in the midst of her literary successes, and Brontë was forced to live in a loveless marriage for the few years before her death. Although "Jane Eyre" ends happily--Jane marries Mr. Rochester--there is still a pervasive sense of darkness and depression in the text as a reflection of Brontë's personal state of mind.

Since its publication, "Jane Eyre" has become a staple of British literature; Brontë's characterization of the honest Jane Eyre, tortured Mr. Rochester, and tragically insane Bertha Mason continue to spur the imagination of readers even today. The novel has inspired several films, as well as numerous literary sequels and prequels (the most famous of which is Jean Rhys' "Wide Sargasso Sea," which describes Mr. Rochester's courtship and marriage to Bertha Mason).

Character List

Jane Eyre

The protagonist and narrator of Jane Eyre, Jane begins the novel as an angry, rebellious, 10-year-old orphan and gradually develops into a sensitive, artistic, maternal, and fiercely independent young woman. In each stage of the novel, Jane is met with fierce opposition from those around her, often because of her low social class and lack of economic independence. Yet, Jane maintains her independent spirit, growing stronger in her beliefs and ideals with each conflict; Jane's inferior position as a governess serves simply to heighten her thirst for independence, both financial and emotional. She rejects marriages to both Mr. Rochester and St. John because she understands she will have to forfeit her independence in the unions. Only after she has attained the financial independence and self-esteem to maintain a marriage of equality does Jane allow herself to marry Mr. Rochester and enjoy a life of love. This self-esteem is gained through Jane's making her mark in various worlds: Lowood, Thornfield, and particularly Moor House, in which she is valued for her humanity and values. Paralleling Jane's desire for independence is her search for a proper set of religious values. She rejects the extremist models of Brocklehurst, Helen Burns, and St. John, and eventually settles on a spirituality of love and connection. The novel ends happily for Jane: not only does she maintain her independence and live with the man she loves, she is able to overcome the social constraints of her position as governess and become a heroine with which every reader can relate.

Edward Rochester

The owner of Thornfield Manor and Jane's lover. Mr. Rochester is an interesting twist on the tragic Byronic hero; though not handsome in a strict sense, his great passion and forcefulness make him an extremely appealing and sensual character in Jane's perspective. Mr. Rochester is also a sympathetic character because of the mistakes he has made in his past: deceived by Bertha Mason's external beauty, Mr. Rochester is constantly brooding and rejecting the darkness of his decision. Despite their difference in backgrounds and social status, Mr. Rochester is a kindred spirit to Jane and feels a sort of emotional peace when he is in her presence. Mr. Rochester is also particularly important to Jane because he provides her with the unconditional love and sense of family that she has never experienced before. Although Mr. Rochester is clearly presented as Jane's superior in intellect and worldly knowledge, the revelation of his marriage to the insane Bertha Mason demonstrates that Jane possesses the moral and ethical superiority in the relationship. Jane rejects his marriage proposal after she learns of Bertha, not only because she feels it would flout the law, but perhaps because Bertha's marriage is a cautionary symbol of Victorian marriage: despite Mr. Rochester's best intentions and Jane's equal intellectual standing, he may still end up imprisoning Jane in his own way through matrimony, just as he has imprisoned Bertha. Ironically, when Jane finally does agree to marry Rochester after having gained her independence, the fire Bertha set to Thornfield has blinded him. Thus, he is suddenly dependent on Jane, a fact which nullifies the typical marriage inequalities of the time period and tips the balance in her favor. On a kinder note, Brontë closes the novel with Mr. Rochester's sight regained in one eye: the marriage is restored to equality and Mr. Rochester and Jane can be happy in their union.

St. John Rivers

The evangelist who takes Jane in at Moor House, brother to Diana and Mary and, it turns out, cousin to Jane. St. John is the last of the three major Christian models Jane observes over the course of the novel. Stoical, cold, and strictly devoted to Christianity, St. John's religion is far too detached for Jane. He refuses to give in to his love for Rosamond Oliver out of a warped sense of duty to God, and Jane concludes that he still knows little about God's love. Although St. John does not love Jane, he believes that she would be suited to missionary work in India and thus, asks her to marry him. While Jane admits that she would gladly accompany him as his cousin (or adopted sister), marrying him under such circumstances would mean forfeiting her rights to a life of passion and love. Losing her autonomy in such a way is unacceptable to her, while accompanying him without marriage violates St. John's sense of propriety. Jane's rejection of St. John's advances seems to spur her return to Rochester, her one chance for spiritual passion. While Rochester is described in terms of fire and flames, St. John is constantly associated with ice and cold, a connection that heightens the lack of passion and joy that would come with a marriage to him. Although the book ends happily for Jane and Mr. Rochester, St. John's ending is far more ambiguous. Although he has traveled to India to fulfill his Christian duty, Bronte still gives the impression that St. John's life could have been more meaningful if he had ever accepted love.

Helen Burns

Jane's friend at Lowood School. Though she dies early on in Jane's time at Lowood, Helen is perhaps the fourth-most important character in the novel for her symbolic value. Upholding the extreme Christian doctrine of tolerance and forgiveness at all costs, Helen serves as a foil to both Mr. Brocklehurst, with his cruel lack of Christian compassion, and Jane, with her anger at those who mistreat her. Helen espouses a Christianity in which faithfulness and compassion are rewarded in Heaven. As an orphan like Jane, Helen believes that her true family is waiting for her in the kingdom of Heaven. With that in mind, she faithfully turns the other cheek when accepting all the cruel punishments handed down at Lowood. She faces especial torments from Mrs. Scratcherd, and, though Helen is distressed by the treatment, she remains unwavering in her beliefs. When Helen dies, Jane absorbs the lesson that the meek shall not inherit the earth. While Jane initially rejects Helen's brand of religion, she does incorporate it in her life later on, especially when she relies on the spiritual kindness of strangers after leaving Thornfield.

Mr. Brocklehurst

The stingy manager of Lowood. Mr. Brocklehurst hypocritically espouses Christian morals in his evangelical sermons and then treats the students at Lowood with disrespect and cruelty. The starvation-level rations and poor condition of the school come in sharp contrast to the luxurious and well-fed existence enjoyed by Brocklehurst's family, and it is discovered that Mr. Brocklehurst has been embezzling school funds to line his own pockets. He is eventually replaced as head of the school.

Mrs. Fairfax

The kindly housekeeper at Thornfield. Distantly related to the Rochesters, Mrs. Fairfax is extremely welcoming to Jane upon her arrival to Thornfield and serves as another surrogate mother for Jane in the novel. She warns Jane against marrying Mr. Rochester because she is concerned about the differences in age and social class. After Jane's departure from Thornfield, Mrs. Fairfax retires with a generous pension from Mr. Rochester.

Bertha Mason

Rochester's insane wife and Richard Mason's sister. A beautiful Creole woman from a prominent West Indies family, Bertha was married to Mr. Rochester in an effort to consolidate the wealth of the two families. Suffering from hereditary insanity that had been kept secret from Mr. Rochester, Bertha began to spiral into madness and violence shortly after their marriage. Eventually, Bertha is imprisoned in the attic at Thornfield under the guard of Grace Poole, a confinement meant to ensure both her own protection and the protection of the other inhabitants of the house. Bertha occasionally escapes from her prison and wreaks havoc in the house; her last outburst involves setting fire to Thornfield and leaping to her own death. As the representation of the classic Gothic figure of "The Madwoman in the Attic," Bertha is both pitiable and terrifying and supports Bronte's critique of gender inequalities and Victorian marriage during the period.

Mrs. Reed

Jane's aunt. Although she promised Mr. Reed that she would treat Jane as her own, Mrs. Reed favors her own spoiled children and harshly punishes Jane for her seeming impudence, even locking her up in the "red-room." When Jane is ten years old, Mrs. Reed sends her to Lowood and then tells John Eyre that Jane has died of typhus fever at the school. On her deathbed, Mrs. Reed reveals that she hated Jane because Mr. Reed loved Jane more than any of his biological children, and she refuses to apologize for mistreating her.

Bessie Lee

A servant at Gateshead. Bessie is Jane's only comfort during her time at Gateshead and occasionally sings her songs and tells her stories. Acting as a surrogate mother for Jane, she is particularly kind after Jane's experience in the red-room and even treats her to a tart on her favorite plate. Bessie visits Jane at Lowood several years after her departure and is impressed with Jane's gentile demeanor. She marries the Gateshead coachman, Robert Leaven, and has three children, the youngest of which she names Jane.

John Reed

Jane's cousin and brother to Eliza and Georgiana. The spoiled darling of his mother, John constantly bullies Jane and is ultimately responsible for her confinement in the red-room at Gateshead. John becomes an alcoholic and avid gambler during his adulthood and commits suicide in order to escape from his massive gambling debts.

Georgiana Reed

Jane's cousin and Eliza's sister. The prettier of the two Reed girls, Georgiana's beauty makes her a spoiled, selfish child, though she befriends Jane as Mrs. Reed dies. She blames Eliza for her failed plans to marry Lord Edwin Vere and shows a similar lack of compassion during her mother's illness. She eventually marries a wealthy man.

Eliza Reed

Jane's cousin and Georgiana's sister. Described by Jane as headstrong and selfish, Eliza is extremely jealous of her sister's beauty and vindictively breaks up Georgiana's engagement to Lord Edwin Vere. She becomes a devout Christian, but, rather than espousing compassion and humanity, she believes only in the importance of "usefulness." After her mother's death, Eliza breaks off all communication with Georgiana and enters a convent in France. She eventually becomes Mother Superior and leaves all of her money to the church.

Adèle Varens

The French-speaking, scampish ward of Mr. Rochester that Jane is hired to tutor. Adèle is the illegitimate child of the opera dancer Céline Varens and an unnamed gentleman. Although she lacks discipline and intellect and suffers from many "French" traits, Adèle improves greatly under Jane's tutelage. She studies at a school of Jane's choosing and grows into a sensible and docile woman who becomes a good companion for Jane.

Grace Poole

Bertha Mason's keeper at Thornfield. As the guard for the third-story prison, Grace's fondness for gin and occasional alcohol-induced naps allow Bertha to escape and wreak havoc in the house, including setting fire to Mr. Rochester's bedchamber, ripping Jane's wedding veil, and causing the fire that destroys Thornfield. Jane is led to believe that the strange goings-on in Thornfield are caused by Grace Poole. It is only after Mr. Briggs and Richard Mason reveal that

Mr. Rochester is already married that Jane understands Grace's true position at Thornfield.

Blanche Ingram

The young and beautiful society lady who is Jane's primary romantic rival. Jane is convinced that the haughty Miss Ingram would be a poor match for Mr. Rochester, but she believes that Mr. Rochester prefers Blanche's beautiful appearance to her own plainness. Mr. Rochester is aware that Blanche is only interested in him for his money, but he pretends that he loves her in order to make Jane jealous. Blanche's comments about governesses during her visit to Thornfield are particularly upsetting to Jane and demonstrate the popular beliefs about governesses during Charlotte Bronte's time.

Miss Temple

The beautiful and kindly superintendent of Lowood. Miss Temple is presented as the foil to the cruel and stingy Mr. Brocklehurst and strives to treat the students at Lowood with as much compassion as possible, even providing them with extra bread and cheese to supplement their meager meals. Miss Temple is particularly kind to Jane and Helen, providing them with seedcake during their tea together and giving Helen a warm bed to die in. As one of the novel's surrogate maternal figures for Jane, Miss Temple demonstrates the lady-like demeanor and inner strength that Jane wishes to possess as an adult.

Céline Varens

Adèle's mother and Mr. Rochester's former mistress. A French opera dancer, Céline pretended to love Rochester but actually only used him for his money. Rochester overhears a conversation between her and one of her other lovers and, filled with rage at his personal humiliation, promptly severs all ties with her. Although Adèle is not his biological daughter, Rochester takes her in as his ward when Céline abandons her to run off to Italy with a musician.

Richard Mason

The brother of Bertha Mason. The handsome but weak-willed man, Richard met Mr. Rochester in the West Indies and encouraged him to marry his beautiful sister without mentioning her hereditary madness. Richard comes to Thornfield in order to check on his sister and is brutally bitten and stabbed by Bertha when he goes to her room alone. When he later learns of Mr. Rochester's bigamous plan to marry Jane, Richard arrives back in England with the solicitor, Mr. Briggs, and stops the marriage.

Diana Rivers

Jane's cousin and the sister of St. John and Mary. Charismatic and independent, Diana is forced to work as a governess in a wealthy household because of her family's financial difficulties. Along with her sister, Diana reveals the injustice of society's treatment of well-bred, intelligent women who are unmarried. Diana supports Jane's decision not to marry St. John and helps Jane to maintain her independence. She marries a navy officer.

Mary Rivers

Jane's cousin and the sister of St. John and Diana Rivers. A strong and independent woman, Mary is forced to work as a governess after her family's loss of wealth. Despite their misfortunes, Mary is kind and compassionate, particularly when Jane begins to live with them at Moor House. Mary and her sister both exemplify the type of independent woman that Jane desires to become. She marries a clergyman.

Mr. Lloyd

The kindly apothecary who suggests Jane attend school at Lowood after her traumatic experience in the red-room at Gateshead. Mr. Lloyd also sends a letter to Miss Temple that clears Jane of Mr. Brocklehurst's charges that she is a liar.

Mr. Briggs

The solicitor from London who publicly reveals Rochester's marriage to Bertha Mason. Briggs is also instrumental in giving Jane her proper inheritance after her uncle dies.

Hannah Rivers

The elderly servant at Moor House. Hannah initially refuses to allow Jane to enter the house because she believes that Jane is a lower-class beggar. Jane chides her for her class prejudices, and the two eventually become good friends.

Rosamond Oliver

The daughter of Mr. Oliver. The beautiful and angelic Rosamond is the benefactress of Jane's school and is overcome with love for St. John. Although he secretly returns her love, St. John cannot allow himself to marry her because of their differing circumstances and his intention to become a missionary. Rosamond ultimately marries the wealthy Mr. Granby.

Mr. Oliver

Rosamond's father. Mr. Oliver is the wealthiest man in Morton and attempts to use his wealth for the benefit of the town, particularly in terms of helping St. John Rivers with his school.

John Eyre

Jane's uncle (as well as the uncle of the Rivers siblings), John made his fortune in wine in Madeira. He intended to adopt Jane but was told that she was dead by Mrs. Reed. Although he dies before they ever meet, John leaves his vast fortune of 20,000 pounds to Jane.

Miss Scatcherd

The history and grammar teacher at Lowood. Miss Scatcherd is generally unkind to her students, but she is particularly cruel and abusive to Helen.

Pilot

Mr. Rochester's faithful dog. Pilot foreshadows Mr. Rochester's presence throughout the book, appearing immediately before Mr. Rochester falls off his horse and maintaining his loyal companionship after Mr. Rochester has lost his eyesight and hand.

Mr. Reed

Jane's other uncle. Because of his great affection for his sister (Jane's mother), Mr. Reed took Jane in when her parents died and intended to raise her with love and kindness. While he was dying, he made Mrs. Reed promise to raise Jane as one of her own, but Mrs. Reed breaks the promise. Although Mr. Reed does not appear as a living character in the novel, Jane constantly feels the presence of his "ghost" during her childhood at Gateshead.

John and Mary

A married couple who works at Thornfield and then cares for Mr. Rochester during his convalescence at Ferndean.

Robert Leaven

The coachman at Gateshead and Bessie's husband. After John Reed's death, Robert comes to Thornfield to bring Jane back to Gateshead with him.

Miss Miller

One of the teachers at Lowood. Miss Miller greets Jane on her initial arrival to the school.

Miss Smith

A teacher at Lowood who instructs the students in sewing.

Madame Pierrot

The French instructor at Lowood.

Miss Gryce

Jane's roommate and fellow teacher at Lowood.

Alice Wood

An orphan who is hired by Rosamond Oliver to assist Jane at the school in Morton.

Major Themes

Family

The main quest in Jane Eyre is Jane's search for family, for a sense of belonging and love. However, this search is constantly tempered by Jane's need for independence. She begins the novel as an unloved orphan who is almost obsessed with finding love as a way to establish her own identity and achieve happiness. Although she does not receive any parental love from Mrs. Reed, Jane finds surrogate maternal figures throughout the rest of the novel. Bessie, Miss Temple, and even Mrs. Fairfax care for Jane and give her the love and guidance that she needs, and she returns the favor by caring for Adèle and the students at her school. Still, Jane does not feel as though she has found her true family until she falls in love with Mr. Rochester at Thornfield; he becomes more of a kindred spirit to her than any of her biological relatives could be. However, she is unable to accept Mr. Rochester's first marriage proposal because she realizes that their marriage - one based on unequal social standing - would compromise her autonomy. Jane similarly denies St. John's marriage proposal, as it would be one of duty, not of passion. Only when she gains financial and emotional autonomy, after having received her inheritance and the familial love of her cousins, can Jane accept Rochester's offer. In fact, the blinded Rochester is more dependent on her (at least until he regains his sight). Within her marriage to Rochester, Jane finally feels completely liberated, bringing her dual quests for family and independence to a satisfying conclusion.

Religion

Jane receives three different models of Christianity throughout the novel, all of which she rejects either partly or completely before finding her own way. Mr. Brocklehurst's Evangelicalism is full of hypocrisy: he spouts off on the benefits of privation and humility while he indulges in a life of luxury and emotionally abuses the students at Lowood. Also at Lowood, Helen Burns's Christianity of absolute forgiveness and tolerance is too meek for Jane's tastes; Helen constantly suffers her punishments silently and eventually dies. St. John, on the other hand, practices a Christianity of utter piousness, righteousness, and principle to the exclusion of any passion. Jane rejects his marriage proposal as much for his detached brand of spirituality as for its certain intrusion on her independence.

However, Jane frequently looks to God in her own way throughout the book, particularly after she learns of Mr. Rochester's previous marriage and before St. John takes her in to Moor House. She also learns to adapt Helen's doctrine of forgiveness without becoming complete passive and returns to Mr. Rochester when she feels that she is ready to accept him again. The culmination of the book is Jane's mystical experience with Mr. Rochester that brings them together through a spirituality of profound love.

Social position

Brontë uses the novel to express her critique of Victorian class differences. Jane is consistently a poor individual within a wealthy environment, particularly with the Reeds and at Thornfield. Her poverty creates numerous obstacles for her and her pursuit of happiness, including personal insecurity and the denial of opportunities. The beautiful Miss Ingram's higher social standing, for instance, makes her Jane's main competitor for Mr. Rochester's love, even though Jane is far superior in terms of intellect and character. Moreover, Jane's refusal to marry Mr. Rochester because of their difference in social stations demonstrates her morality and belief in the importance of personal independence, especially in comparison to Miss Ingram's gold-digging inclinations. Although Jane asserts that her poverty does not make her an inferior person, her eventual ascent out of poverty does help her overcome her personal obstacles. Not only does she generously divide her inheritance with her cousins, but her financial independence solves her difficulty with low self-esteem and allows her to fulfill her desire to be Mr. Rochester's wife.

Gender inequality

Alongside Brontë's critique of Victorian class hierarchy is a subtler condemnation of the gender inequalities during the time period. The novel begins with Jane's imprisonment in the "red-room" at Gateshead, and later in the book Bertha's imprisonment in the attic at Thornfield is revealed. The connection implies that Jane's imprisonment is symbolic of her lower social class, while Bertha's containment is symbolic of Victorian marriage: all women, if they marry under unequal circumstances as Bertha did, will eventually be confined and oppressed by their husbands in some manner. Significantly, Jane is consciously aware of the problems associated with unequal marriages. Thus, even though she loves Mr. Rochester, she refuses to marry him until she has her own fortune and can enter into the marriage contract as his equal.

While it is difficult to separate Jane's economic and gender obstacles, it is clear that her position as a woman also prevents her from venturing out into the world as many of the male characters do – Mr. Rochester, her Uncle John, and St. John, for instance. Indeed, her desire for worldly experience makes her last name ironic, as "Eyre" derives from an Old French word meaning "to travel." If Jane were a man, Brontë suggests, she would not be forced to submit to so much economic hardship; she could actively attempt to make her fortune. As it is, however, Jane must work as a governess, the only legitimate position open for a woman of her station, and simply wait for her uncle to leave her his fortune.

Fire and Ice

The motifs of fire and ice permeate the novel from start to finish. Fire is presented as positive, creative, and loving, while ice is seen as destructive, negative, and hateful. Brontë highlights this dichotomy by associating these distinct elements with particular characters: the cruel or detached characters, such as Mrs. Reed and

St. John, are associated with ice, while the warmer characters, such as Jane, Miss Temple, and Mr. Rochester, are linked with fire. Interestingly, fire serves as a positive force even when it is destructive, as when Jane burns Helen's humiliating "Slattern" crown, and when Bertha sets fire to Mr. Rochester's bed curtains and then to Thornfield Manor. The first of Bertha's fires brings Jane and Mr. Rochester into a more intimate relationship, while the second destroys Thornfield and leads to Bertha's death, thus liberating Rochester from his shackled past. Although the fire also blinds Rochester, this incident helps Jane see that he is now dependent on her and erases any misgivings she may have about inequality in their marriage. Although Brontë does not suggest that the characters associated with ice are wholly malignant or unsympathetic, she emphasizes the importance of fiery love as the key to personal happiness.

Gothic elements

Brontë uses many elements of the Gothic literary tradition to create a sense of suspense and drama in the novel. First of all, she employs Gothic techniques in order to set the stage for the narrative. The majority of the events in the novel take place within a gloomy mansion (Thornfield Manor) with secret chambers and a mysterious demonic laugh belonging to the Madwoman in the Attic. Brontë also evokes a sense of the supernatural, incorporating the terrifying ghost of Mr. Reed in the red-room and creating a sort of telepathic connection between Jane and Mr. Rochester. More importantly, however, Brontë uses the Gothic stereotype of the Byronic hero to formulate the primary conflict of the text. Brooding and tortured, while simultaneously passionate and charismatic, Mr. Rochester is the focal point of the passionate romance in the novel and ultimately directs Jane's behavior beginning at her time at Thornfield. At the same time, his dark past and unhappy marriage to Bertha Mason set the stage for the dramatic conclusion of the novel.

External beauty versus internal beauty

Throughout the novel, Brontë plays with the dichotomy between external beauty and internal beauty. Both Bertha Mason and Blanche Ingram are described as stunningly beautiful, but, in each case, the external beauty obscures an internal ugliness. Bertha's beauty and sensuality blinded Mr. Rochester to her hereditary madness, and it was only after their marriage that he gradually recognized her true nature. Blanche's beauty hides her haughtiness and pride, as well as her desire to marry Mr. Rochester only for his money. Yet, in Blanche's case, Mr. Rochester seems to have learned not to judge by appearances, and he eventually rejects her, despite her beauty. Only Jane, who lacks the external beauty of typical Victorian heroines, has the inner beauty that appeals to Mr. Rochester. Her intelligence, wit, and calm morality express a far greater personal beauty than that of any other character in the novel, and Brontë clearly intends to highlight the importance of personal development and growth rather than superficial appearances. Once Mr. Rochester loses his hand and eyesight, they are also on equal footing in terms of appearance: both must look beyond superficial qualities in order to love each other.

Glossary of Terms

abode
home

acrid
irritating to the senses

acrimonious
bitter in nature

affable
pleasant

aloof
reserved or indifferent

analogous
similar

animadversion
strong disapproval

antipathy
strong dislike or aversion

aperture
a small opening, i.e. crack or hole

artifice
trickery

ascendancy
domination or control

aspirant
an individual who hopes

assiduous
diligent and attentive

austere
severe or serious

aversion
a strong feeling of dislike

azure
light blue

bane
a source of ruin

becalmed
to make motionless through lack of wind

benignant
kind

bilious
irritable

billow
to swell or rise

bleak
dreary and desolate

bleared
blurry

brackish
salty

burgh
an incorporated town with some degree of independence

calico
a cotton fabric with a printed pattern

canzonette
a song for voice and accompaniment

captious
difficult to please

caviller
an individual who makes unnecessary and irritating objections

celerity
speed

censure
a strong statement of disapproval

cessation
stopping

charnel
a room in which dead bodies and bones are deposited

chiding
scolding

chintz
a printed cotton fabric

choler
anger

civility
politeness

coax
to persuade sweetly

congeal
to solidify

consecration
blessing given by a sacred office

conspicuous
easily noticed

consternation
amazement or fear that causes confusion

consumption
a nineteenth-century term for tuberculosis

conveyance
the act of transporting; also, communication

convolvuli
any plant belonging to the Morning Glory family, characterized by twining plants and trumpet-shaped flowers

cordiality
friendliness

cormorant
a type of seabird

corporeal
bodily

covet
to desire wrongfully

croquant
a cake made from crisp pastry

cumbrous
unwieldy or bulky

damask
a lustrous fabric with satin patterns

dexterous
skillful

diablerie
witchcraft

diffidence

shyness

dispense
to deal out

disposition
personality

docile
mild or gentle

dreg
a small amount

ecclesiastical
relating to the church

effigy
an image or likeness

effluence
an outward flow

effluvia
a vapor, often an unpleasant one

cnigma
mystery

equipage
a carriage drawn by horses

etiolated
to drain of color or life

evince
to display

execration
the act of cursing

exigency
urgency

fagging
exhausting

fastidious
very particular or demanding

ferret out
to discover

fervid
fiery

fervour
warmth of feeling

festoon
a decorative garland

fetid
foul-smelling

flaxen
a pale, yellow color, i.e. corresponding to the color of flax

flog
to beat

forlorn
unhappy or depressed

fury
a violent woman

gaunt
bony

girdle
a sash worn at the waist

gradation
a process that goes through a series of degrees or stages

gregarious
outgoing

hamlet
a small town

hardy
sturdy

hebdomadal
occurring every seven days

heterogeneous
varied

hiatus
a break or pause

holland
a cotton cloth with an opaque finish

homily
a sermon

humble
lowly or inferior

ignominious
humiliating

imbibe
to consume or absorb

imperious
masterful

impromptu
not rehearsed

impudent
disrespectful

incredulous
unbelieving

indefatigable
untiring

indemnity
protection against damage

indigence
poverty

inestimable
priceless

inferiority
lower in status or position

influx
flowing in

ingenuous
innocent or naive

insuperable
impossible to overcome

interlocutrice
a female individual who takes part in a conversation

irate
angry

ire
wrath

irid
iris of the eye

irksome
annoying

judicious
sensible

lamentable
regrettable

licence
British spelling of the term "license

limpid
clear

lineaments
a feature of the face or body

lurid
hideous

manifestation
demonstration

mediatrix
a woman who mediates between two groups

mercenary
an individual who acts solely for money or reward

meridian
the highest point or culmination

merino
wool from a particular breed of sheep

mien
manner or presence

moreen
a heavy wool or cotton fabric

mullioned
a vertical division between a window or door

muslin
a cotton fabric, often printed or embroidered

mutiny
an uprising against authority

noxious
dangerous

obtrusive
pushy

obviate
avoid or ward off

opaque
unclear or concealed

opprobrious
shameful

orthodox
traditional

ostensible
superficial

paltry
very small

pelisse
a woman's long cloak

penality
an act involving punishment

pendent
hanging

penurious
cheap

peremptory
imperious or commanding in tone

perfidy
disloyalty or treachery

peruse
to study carefully

pervious
open to argument or reason

pettish
disagreeable

petulant
grouchy

physiognomy
the face or outward appearance

piety
reverence for God

pinafore
a child's apron

piquant
lively

poltroon
coward

prattle
chatter

precocious
unusually mature in development or intelligence

presentiment
foreboding

preternatural
abnormal

privation
a state of hardship or need

promontory
a bluff or peak

pungent
biting or sharp to the senses

quaint
picturesque

rancid
rotten

redolent
fragrant

redundant
unnecessary repetition

repast
meal

repletion
fullness from food or drink

resurgam
a Latin term meaning, "I shall rise again"

retaliation
an act of revenge or repayment

reverberation
an echo

ribaldry
characterized by crudeness or vulgarity

rigor
severity

rill
a small brook

ruddy
having a healthy red color

ruth
pity

salient
prominent or eye-catching

sallow
a sickly yellow complexion

salubrious
healthful

sanguine
optimistic or cheerful

scapegoat
an individual blamed for the actions of another

scrutinize
to examine closely

sentient
conscious or aware of the senses

sequester
to separate or move into seclusion

shrubbery
a group of bushes or shrubs

skein
a coil of yarn or thread

slatternly
untidy

solace
comfort

sombre
dark and depressing

soporific
characterized by sleepiness

spar
to dispute or argue

sprightly
lively

stagnation
to become idle and unchanging

sublunary
characterized by the earth; also, mundane

supplication
plea

surtout
a woman's hood

sweetmeats
any type of candied delicacy, often made with fruit and nuts

tabernacle
a place of worship

tenacious
stubborn

thwart
to defeat or frustrate

timorous
fearful

torpid
dull or sluggish

torpor
inactivity or laziness

totter
stagger

transient
temporary

truculent
hostile

tucker
a piece of linen or muslin worn around a woman's shoulders

tumult
a noisy outbreak or disturbance

turbulent
stormy

typhus fever
an infectious disease characterized by a headache and red spots on the skin

uncongenial
unpleasant

unimpeachable
faultless

usury
lending money with an excessive rate of interest

vermilion
bright red

visage
face

zealous
dedicated

Short Summary

Ten-year-old orphan Jane Eyre lives unhappily with her wealthy relatives, the Reed family, at Gateshead. Resentful of the late Mr. Reed's preference for her, Jane's aunt and cousins take every opportunity to neglect and abuse her as a reminder of her inferior station. Jane's only salvation from her daily humiliations is Bessie, the kindly servant who tells her stories and sings her songs. One day, Jane confronts her bullying cousin, John, and Mrs. Reed punishes her by imprisoning her in the "red-room," the room in which her uncle died. Convinced that she sees her uncle's ghost, Jane faints. When she awakes, Jane is being cared for the apothecary, Mr. Lloyd, who suggests that she be sent off to school. Mrs. Reed is happy to be rid of her troublesome charge and immediately sends Jane to the Lowood School, an institution fifty miles from Gateshead.

Jane soon discovers that life at the Lowood School is bleak, particularly because of the influence of the hypocritical headmaster, Mr. Brocklehurst, whose cruelty and evangelical self-righteousness results in poor conditions, inedible meals, and frequent punishments for the students. During an inspection of the school, Mr. Brocklehurst humiliates Jane by forcing to stand on a stool in the middle of the class and accusing her of being a liar. The beautiful superintendent, Miss Temple, believes in Jane's innocence and writes to Mr. Lloyd for clarification of Jane's nature. Although Jane continues to suffer privations in the austere environment, Miss Temple's benevolence encourages her to devote herself to her studies.

While at Lowood, Jane also befriends Helen Burns, who upholds a doctrine of Christian forgiveness and tolerance. Helen is constantly mistreated by Miss Scratcherd, one of the more unpleasant teachers at the school, but maintains her passivity and "turns the other cheek." Although Jane is unable to accept Helen's doctrine completely – her passionate nature cannot allow her to endure mistreatment silently– Jane attempts to mirror Helen's patience and calmness in her own character. During the spring, an outbreak of typhus fever ravages the school, and Helen dies of consumption in Jane's arms. The deaths by typhus alert the benefactors to the school's terrible conditions, and it is revealed that Mr. Brocklehurst has been embezzling school funds in order to provide for his own luxurious lifestyle. After Mr. Brocklehurst's removal, Jane's time at Lowood is spent more happily and she excels as a student for six years and as a teacher for two.

Despite her security at Lowood, Jane is dissatisfied and yearns for new adventures. She accepts a position as governess at Thornfield Manor and is responsible for teaching a vivacious French girl named Adèle. In addition to Adèle, Jane spends much of her time at Thornfield with Mrs. Fairfax, the elderly housekeeper who runs the estate during the master's absence. Jane also begins to notice some mysterious happenings around Thornfield, including the master's constant absence from home and the demonic laugh that Jane hears emanating from the third-story attic.

After much waiting, Jane finally meets her employer, Edward Rochester, a brooding, detached man who seems to have a dark past. Although Mr. Rochester is not handsome in the traditional sense, Jane feels an immediate attraction to him based on their intellectual communion. One night, Jane saves Mr. Rochester from a fire in his bedroom, which he blames on Grace Poole, a seamstress with a propensity for gin. Because Grace continues to work at Thornfield, Jane decides that Mr. Rochester has withheld some important information about the incident.

As the months go by, Jane finds herself falling more and more in love with Mr. Rochester, even after he tells her of his lustful liaison with Adèle's mother. However, Jane becomes convinced that Mr. Rochester would never return her affection when he brings the beautiful Blanche Ingram to visit at Thornfield. Though Rochester flirts with the idea of marrying Miss Ingram, he is aware of her financial ambitions for marriage. During Miss Ingram's visit, an old acquaintance of Rochester's, Richard Mason, also visits Thornfield and is severely injured from an attack - apparently by Grace - in the middle of the night in the attic. Jane, baffled by the circumstances, tends to him, and Rochester confesses to her that he made an error in the past that he hopes to overturn by marrying Miss Ingram. He says that he has another governess position for Jane lined up elsewhere.

Jane returns to Gateshead for a few weeks to see the dying Mrs. Reed. Mrs. Reed still resents Jane and refuses to apologize for mistreating her as a child; she also admits that she lied to Jane's uncle, John Eyre, and told him that she had died during the typhus outbreak at Lowood. When Jane returns to Thornfield, Rochester tells her that he knows Miss Ingram's true motivations for marriage, and he asks Jane to marry him. Jane accepts, but a month later, Mason and a solicitor, Mr. Briggs, interrupt the wedding ceremony by revealing that Rochester already has a wife: Mason's sister, Bertha, who is kept in the attic in Thornfield under the care of Grace Poole. Rochester confesses his past misdeeds to Jane. In his youth he needed to marry the wealthy Bertha for money, but was unaware of her family's history of madness. Despite his best efforts to help her, Bertha eventually descended into a state of complete madness that only her imprisonment could control. Jane still loves Mr. Rochester, but she cannot allow herself to become his mistress: she leaves Thornfield.

Penniless and devastated by Mr. Rochester's revelations, Jane is reduced to begging for food and sleeping outdoors. Fortunately, the Rivers siblings, St. John (pronounced "Sinjin"), Diana, and Mary, take her into their home at Moor House and help her to regain her strength. Jane becomes close friends with the family, and quickly develops a great affection for the ladies. Although the stoically religious St. John is difficult to approach, he finds Jane a position working as a teacher at a school in Morton. One day, Jane learns that she has inherited a vast fortune of 20,000 pounds from her uncle, John Eyre. Even more surprising, Jane discovers that the Rivers siblings are actually her cousins. Jane immediately decides to share her newfound wealth with her relatives.

St. John is going to go on missionary work in India and repeatedly asks Jane to accompany him as his wife. She refuses, since it would mean compromising her capacity for passion in a loveless marriage. Instead, she is drawn to thoughts of Mr. Rochester and, one day, after experiencing a mystical connection with him, seeks him out at Thornfield. She discovers that the estate has been burned down by Bertha, who died in the fire, and that Mr. Rochester, who lost his eyesight and one of his hands in the fire, lives at the nearby estate of Ferndean. He is overjoyed when she locates him, and relates his side of the mystical connection that Jane had. He and Jane soon marry. At the end of the novel, Jane informs the readers that she and Mr. Rochester have been married for ten years, and Mr. Rochester regained sight in one of his eyes in time to see the birth of his first son.

Quotes and Analysis

God and nature intended you for a missionary's wife. It is not personal, but mental endowments they have given you: you are formed for labour, not for love. A missionary's wife you must - shall be. You shall be mine: I claim you - not for my pleasure, but for my Sovereign's service.

St. John Rivers

St. John makes this statement when he is attempting to convince Jane to marry him and become a missionary in India. St. John's declaration that Jane is formed for "labour, not for love" emphasizes his belief that love and passion have no place in a moral life. St. John's argument of ownership also highlights his view of Jane as a subservient companion, not a woman with independent thoughts. Although Jane approves of St. John's morality, she is unwilling to sacrifice love to become the kind of woman that St. John wants her to be.

There was no possibility of taking a walk that day. We had been wandering, indeed, in the leafless shrubbery an hour in the morning; but since dinner (Mrs. Reed, when there was no company, dined early) the cold winter wind had brought with it clouds so sombre, and a rain so penetrating, that further out-door exercise was now out of the question. I was glad of it: I never liked long walks, especially on chilly afternoons: dreadful to me was the coming home in the raw twilight, with nipped fingers and toes, and a heart saddened by the chidings of Bessie, the nurse, humbled by the consciousness of my physical inferiority to Eliza, John, and Georgiana Reed.

Jane Eyre

This is one of the more famous quotations from the novel because it provides an immediate sense of Jane's personality, as well as her position of lonely inferiority among her cousins at Gateshead. In the first line, it seems as if Jane desires to take a walk and is upset that she cannot. However, with the addition of the later lines, it becomes clear that Jane actually dislikes long walks - even from the very beginning of the novel, Bronte informs the readers that Jane is an atypical character who will make some surprising decisions. This opening quotation also describes the extent of Jane's loneliness and unhappiness with the Reed family; it is because of her empty childhood that Jane thirsts for the family and love that she will find with Mr. Rochester at Thornfield Manor.

I knew you would do me good in some way, at some time; - I saw it in your eyes when I first beheld you: their expression and smile did not - did not strike delight to my very inmost heart so for nothing. People talk of natural sympathies: I have heard of good genii: - there are grains of truth in the wildest fable. My cherished preserver, good-night!

Edward Rochester

This quotation occurs immediately after Bertha Mason has set Mr. Rochester's bed on fire and Jane has rescued him. Mr. Rochester discards his sarcasm for one of the first times in the novel and acknowledges that he feels a significant emotional connection to Jane. This intimate moment is only possible because of Mr. Rochester's vulnerable position, and both the reader and Jane begin to see some of the person who lives beneath his brooding and tormented exterior. Bronte will continue to explore the idea that Jane and Mr. Rochester are kindred spirits as the novel continues, but even these few lines lay the seeds for the fiery passion that will pervade Jane's relationship with Mr. Rochester.

I am very happy, Jane; and when you hear that I am dead you must be sure and not grieve: there is nothing to grieve about. We all must die one day, and the illness which is removing me is not painful; it is gentle and gradual: my mind is at rest. I leave no one to regret me much: I have only a father; and he is lately married, and will not miss me. By dying young I shall escape great sufferings. I had not qualities or talents to make my way very well in the world: I should have been continually at fault.

Helen Burns

This speech comes when Helen Burns is dying in Jane's arms at Lowood School. Although she only appears for a few chapters, Helen and her view of Christianity become very significant to Jane as she grows into adulthood. Helen argued for turning the other cheek: accepting the injustice and unhappiness of the earthly world because of the joys that await in heaven. Although Jane does not wholly agree with Helen's passivity, particularly in the face of the torments at Lowood, she admires Helen's strength of faith. Still, Jane fears for her friend's death and the inevitable loneliness that will come when she is gone. Helen strives to convince Jane not to be unhappy because she is finally fulfilling her destiny and finding peace with God.

Reader, I married him. A quiet wedding we had: he and I, the parson and clerk, were alone present.

Jane Eyre

This quotation comes after Jane has gone to Ferndean and discovered the newly-blinded Mr. Rochester. Up until this point in the text, Jane has always maintained a subservient position to Mr. Rochester. However, with the inheritance from her uncle, Jane is now an independent woman and can take charge of her own destiny. Moreover, with the loss of Mr. Rochester's eyesight, he becomes vulnerable and dependent on Jane; he can no longer maintain his former position as the superior male. Thus, instead of using the subservient "He married me," in which Mr. Rochester is the dominating partner, Jane takes the superior in the relationship: "I married him." However, this inequality is resolved when Mr. Rochester regains the use of one of his eyes; Jane and Mr. Rochester are finally able to support a relationship of mutual respect and quality.

You never felt jealousy, did you, Miss Eyre? Of course not: I need not ask you; because you never felt love. You have both sentiments yet to experience: your soul sleeps; the shock is yet to be given which shall waken it.

Edward Rochester

This speech occurs when Mr. Rochester tells Jane about Adele's origins and his affair with Celine Varens. Mr. Rochester's assertion that Jane has never felt love is not necessarily false. At this point in her sheltered life, Jane has barely experienced familial love, not to mention romantic love. Mr. Rochester's conclusion about Jane's emotional experience also emphasizes her inferior position in their relationship. Because he has experienced many kinds of love, Mr. Rochester is ultimately wiser and thus, superior to his naive governess. However, Bronte suggests that Jane actually possesses far more wisdom and clarity about love that Mr. Rochester: she is the only one of the two who is able to resist the call of animal passion and resist the temptation to become his mistress.

Why, I suppose you have a governess for her: I saw a person with her just now - is she gone? Oh, no! there she is still behind the window-curtain. You pay her, of course: I should think it quite as expensive, - more so; for you have them both to keep in addition...You should hear mama on the chapter of governesses: Mary and I have had, I should think, a dozen at least in our day; half of them detestable and the rest ridiculous, and all incubi - were they not, mama?

Blanche Ingram

Jane overhears this speech by Blanche Ingram during one of the social gatherings at Thornfield. Blanche expresses the upper-class prejudice against governesses and other members of the lower-class. Instead of respecting governesses for the work that they must do, Blanches mocks them openly and without any consideration for Jane's presence in the room. In her mind, a governess is nothing more than a servant and worthy of even less respect. This attitude is one that Jane constantly faces as a governess; Mr. Rochester is the only member of high society who ever treats her with respect.

She bit me. She worried me like a tigress, when Rochester got the knife from her...She sucked the blood: she said she'd drain my heart.

Richard Mason

This speech takes place after Richard Mason has been attacked by Bertha. Although Mr. Rochester forbids Jane and Richard Mason to speak about what has occurred, Jane cannot help overhearing this clue to the mystery of Thornfield. Through Mason's description, Bronte is able to present Bertha's nature as bestial (as a tigress) and even vampiric, a term in itself that alludes to the Gothic literary tradition. Not only is Bertha akin to the animal world in all its chaos, she is even carnivorous and attempts to suck the life out of her brother in the same way that her presence threatens to suck the life out of Mr. Rochester's happiness with Jane. Bertha's uncontrollable animal nature comes in stark contrast to Jane's placidity and rationality; although Jane possesses some of the same fiery passion that Bertha has, Jane is able to control her inclinations with her humanity.

If people were always kind and obedient to those who are cruel and unjust, the wicked people would have it all their own way: they would never feel afraid, and so they would never alter, but would grow worse and worse. When we are struck at without a reason, we should strike back again very hard; I am sure we should - so hard as to teach the person who struck us never to do it again.

Jane Eyre

This speech occurs during one of Jane's conversations with Helen Burns at Lowood. Although Helen prescribes to the idea of "turning the other cheek" when mistreated, Jane believes that people should defend themselves to ensure that they are never mistreated again. Jane is unable to mirror Helen's passivity at Lowood and her passion and strength of character will help her to overcome many obstacles in her life. Eventually Jane learns to hide her passion and anger at injustice, but Mr. Rochester will still recognize a kindred spirit beneath her calm exterior.

You must be on your guard against her; you must shun her example: if necessary, avoid her company, exclude her from your sports, and shut her out from your converse. Teachers, you must watch her: keep your eyes on her movements, weight well her words, scrutinize her actions, punish her body to saver her soul; if indeed, such salvation be possible for (my tongue falters while I tell it) this girl, this child, the native of a Christian land, worse than many a little heathen who says its prayers to Brahma and kneels before Juggernaut - this girl is - a liar!

Mr. Brocklehurst

Mr. Brocklehurst represents the worst kind of Christianity in the novel. His evangelical sermons, extreme stinginess, and cruel treatment of his students come in sharp contrast with his family's luxurious lifestyle and his embezzlement of school funds. In this particular scene, Mr. Brocklehurst demonstrates the extent of his cruelty by tormenting Jane with false accusations in front of her school peers. Although Mr. Brocklehurst is eventually removed from his position at Lowood, he remains one of the worst obstacles that the child Jane must overcome in order to continue her quest for independence.

Summary and Analysis of Volume I, Chapters 1-5

Volume I, Chapter 1 Summary:

The novel begins with the ten-year-old Jane Eyre narrating from the home of the well-off Reed family in Gateshead Hall. Mr. Reed, Jane's uncle, took her into his home after both of her parents died of typhus fever, but he soon died himself. Mrs. Reed was particularly resentful of her husband's favoritism toward Jane and takes every opportunity to neglect and punish her. At the beginning of the narrative, Jane is secluded behind the curtains of a window seat and reading Bewick's "History of British Birds." Although she attempted to join the rest of the family, she was refused permission by Mrs. Reed to play with her cousins Eliza, John, and Georgiana. Although the family mistreats her, Jane still wishes that she could have the same attention and love that her cousins receive from her aunt. The bullying John interrupts Jane's reading and informs her that she has no right to read their books because she is an orphan who is dependent on his family. He strikes her with the book, and Jane surprises him by fighting to defend herself. John is frightened by Jane's zeal and blames her for the fight. As punishment for Jane's inappropriate behavior, Mrs. Reed has two servants lock her in the "red-room," the room in which Mr. Reed died.

Analysis:

From the very beginning of the book, Bronte uses careful novelistic craftsmanship to position the reader on Jane's side. Not only does the narration occur in Jane's voice, a fact which automatically makes her a more sympathetic character, but Bronte incorporates all of the tragic facts of Jane's childhood in the first few pages. From the start, Jane is oppressed; she is sent off while her cousins play. We learn through exposition from John that she is a penniless orphan, dependent on the heartless Reed family but never on an equal level with her relatives; indeed, social class will play an important role in the rest of the novel. Although we do not have a clear sense of the extent of Mrs. Reed's resentful feelings toward Jane, Bronte emphasizes Jane's loneliness and lack of familial affection. Bronte also emphasizes Jane's sensitive nature and inner strength. She is given to flights of fancy while reading, but she also displays a great deal of courage and sense of justice in her defense against John. All of the elements are in place for a classic "Bildungsroman," the literary genre originating in the German as "novel of formation" or, as it is generally known, the "coming-of-age" story. In the Bildungsroman, classic examples of which are Goethe's The Sorrows of Young Werther, Mark Twain's Huckleberry Finn, and J.D. Salinger's The Catcher in the Rye, the young protagonist matures through a series of obstacles and defines his or her identity.

Volume I, Chapter 2 Summary:

Jane resists physically and verbally as the servants Bessie and Miss Abbot lead her to the red-room, named for the color of its drapery and furniture. The room also contains a miniature portrait of Mr. Reed, who has been dead nine years; his actual body lies in a vault under the Gateshead church. Before they lock her up, the servants reprimand Jane for her disobedience and warn her against angering God. As Jane considers their reprimands, she becomes angry at the injustice of her family situation, wondering why she is always mistreated while her cousins are pampered and petted. She catches her ghostly reflection in the mirror and, thinking about her miserable condition and about her dead uncle, recalls how he took the orphaned Jane in and made Mrs. Reed promise to take care of her. Suddenly, a ray of light enters the room, and Jane cries out, believing that the light is the ghost of her uncle. Her scream of terror alerts Bessie, Miss Abbot, and Mrs. Reed, but they accuse her of trickery and refuse to free her. After they leave, Jane faints.

Analysis:

The red-room has clear associations with death (red as the color of blood, the room's containing a miniature version of the dead Mr. Reed, and Jane's belief that she sees a ghost in it) but is also a symbol of imprisonment. This is only the first time that Jane will be imprisoned in the novel, though her later imprisonments will generally be more metaphorical, particularly in relation to class, gender, and religion. In this case, John is the root cause of Jane's imprisonment and his word is taken above hers, a fact that parallels the gender relations of the male dominated Victorian society. Ironically, however, the three aggressors that maintain Jane's imprisonment in the red-room are females, and Jane's one savior, it appears, was her uncle.

The chapter also introduces some of the Gothic literary tradition that inform much of the narrative structure of the text. The Gothic novel, popularized in the 18th-century, utilizes supernatural, suspenseful, and mysterious settings and events to create an atmosphere of horror and morbidity. With that in mind, the ominous quality of the red-room, the ghost that Jane thinks she sees and the revelation that Mr. Reed's body lies beneath the church each contribute to the horror that Jane feels at her imprisonment. The Gothic novel is also characterized by damsels in distress (and women are frequently the protagonists); though Jane faints here, common for Gothic women, she proves herself to be strong-willed and determined to fight back against her oppressors.

Volume I, Chapter 3 Summary:

Jane wakes up, dimly aware of voices and of someone supporting her. She soon realizes that she is in her bed and sees Bessie and Mr. Lloyd, the apothecary. He gives instructions for Jane's care and departs, and Bessie, more concerned than before over Jane's health, sleeps in the neighboring room in case Jane needs anything during the night. Jane sleeps and awakens the next day feeling terrible. The Reed family is away, and Bessie brings Jane a fruit tart and her favorite book, "Gulliver's Travels." Yet, Jane still feels so distressed from her experience in the red-room that she is unable to eat the tart or even enjoy the fantastical tales of "Gulliver's Travels" as she normally does. She cries after Bessie sings her a sad song (a popular one composed by Edward Ransford, c. 1840) about an orphan.

Mr. Lloyd returns and, once Bessie is gone, Jane tries to tell him about the ghost of Mr. Reed that she saw. He does not believe her, and whenever she brings up the abuses she suffers at Gateshead, he observes that she is lucky to live in such a beautiful house. Jane thinks that she has some poor relatives, but, after Mr. Lloyd's prompting, admits that she would not like to live with them, even if they were kind. Mr. Lloyd then asks her if she would like to go to school. After some contemplation, Jane concludes that school would be an improvement over Gateshead, and she begins to be excited about the possibility.

The family returns, and Mr. Lloyd speaks with Mrs. Reed with the recommendation of sending Jane to school. Later, while pretending to be asleep, Jane overhears Miss Abbot and Bessie discussing her parent's history. Jane's mother was a member of the wealthy Reed family but was cut off financially when she married a poor clergyman against the wishes of her father. Soon after Jane's birth, her parents died of typhus while visiting poor people in a manufacturing town. Miss Abbot and Bessie admit that Jane's background is a tragic one, but admit that it would be easier to pity her if she were a pretty, likable child.

Analysis:

The conflicts of social class that were suggested in Chapter 1 become even more prominent in this chapter. Jane is trapped in the odd situation of being poor within a rich family. Moreover, her mother was once a member of a wealthy family, but her choice of husband resulted in her financial ruin and indirectly led to both of their deaths. As such, Jane's notions of poverty are fundamentally skewed; as she admits, children "have not much idea of industrious, working, respectable poverty - poverty for me was synonymous with degradation." Even though she is unhappy at Gateshead, she freely admits to Mr. Lloyd that she would rather be mistreated in a wealthy home than treated kindly among poor people.

Adding insult to injury, Bessie's song, well-meaning though it may have been, emphasizes Jane's status as a "poor orphan child" and isolation in the Reed family. Jane, of course, is poor in both pitiable and pecuniary terms, without anyone to love her and without any money for self-sufficiency. However, Mr. Lloyd's suggestion about going to school is intriguing, particularly because an education was the one thing that could help a woman strive for financial independence in the Victorian era.

Volume I, Chapter 4 Summary:

Time passes, and Jane regains her strength, but the subject of her unhappiness is never broached, and the Reed family treats her even more poorly than before. One day, Jane challenges Mrs. Reed, questioning what her late husband would think of her behavior. Mrs. Reed punishes Jane for the impertinent question, boxing her ears and ordering Bessie to lecture her, but Jane is interested in the sudden look of fear that she detected in her aunt's eyes. When the holidays arrive, Jane continues to be excluded from family celebrations and finds solace only in the doll with which she sleeps and in Bessie's kindly goodnight kisses. In mid-January, Mr. Brocklehurst, whose Lowood School Jane learns she will attend, visits Gateshead and interrogates Jane about her religious beliefs. When Jane informs him that she finds the Psalms to be uninteresting, Mr. Brocklehurst warns her that such beliefs are a sign of wickedness, and she must repent and cleanse her "wicked heart." Mrs. Reed tells Mr. Brocklehurst that she hopes that Jane's time at Lowood will reform her, particularly her tendency to lie, an accusation that stings Jane. After Mr. Brocklehurst leaves, Jane defends her honesty to her aunt and launches a series of recriminations. Mrs. Reed seems stunned and leaves the room, but Jane's victorious feelings soon give way to remorse. She feels better later when Bessie confides in her that she prefers Jane to the other children.

Analysis:

Religion makes its first formal appearance in the novel in the form of Mr. Brocklehurst. Already, we can see the religious hypocrisies that Bronte exposes; Mr. Brocklehurst believes the deceitful Mrs. Reed's accusations about Jane and relishes the seemingly heartless reformations that take place at school. He also displays an abhorrence for any form of creative thinking; although Jane enjoys Revelations, the book of Daniel, Genesis, and other parts of the Bible, she is accused of being "wicked" because she does not approve of the Psalms. The extent of Mr. Brocklehurst's hypocrisy in his beliefs about Christianity will become more apparent in later chapters of the novel.

After the night in the red-room, Jane's position in the Reed family seems to have fallen even further. Instead of being tormented by Georgiana, Eliza, and John, as she was before, Jane is now simply ignored; she no longer even exists in the context of the family. However, Jane does find comfort in Bessie, who begins to act as a surrogate mother figure and is Jane's only source of consolation and affection. Although Bessie seemed to be harsh at earlier points in the novel, her sole support of Jane during this time (and acknowledgement that she prefers Jane over the other children), make Mrs. Reed's antipathy toward Jane seem increasingly callous. Bessie's behavior toward Jane and Jane's love for her doll both constitute one of the major themes of the novel, the idea that "human beings must love something."

In this chapter, Bronte also introduces the motif of fire and ice, a theme that will appear frequently throughout the novel. Fire is associated with Jane and with positive creation, while ice is associated with Jane's antagonists and with negative destruction. Bronte is often subtle with these symbolic attachments; for example, Mrs. Reed's eyes are twice compared to ice in this chapter: "her cold, composed grey eyes" and "her eye of ice continued to dwell freezingly on mine."

Volume I, Chapter 5 Summary:

Four days after meeting Mr. Brocklehurst, Jane leaves Gateshead by the 6am coach for Lowood School. When she arrives at the school, she is taken into a dull, grey room for supper and then put to bed in a room filled with other girls. The next day, Jane is introduced to some of the school's daily routines, which consist of Bible recitations, regular academic lessons, and abominable meals. She also meets the kindly, beautiful superintendent, Miss Temple, and another girl, Helen Burns, who informs Jane that all the student are "charity-children" - orphans whose tuition is largely made up for by benefactors. Jane realizes that Mrs. Reed has not paid anything to support her at Lowood, and she is truly without any family. Jane also observes one of the nastier teachers, Miss Scatcherd, mistreating Helen in class. Much to her surprise, the stoic Helen impressively bears her punishment without complaint.

Analysis:

Immediately we see that Lowood's religious education does not necessarily mean that the orphans are treated well. Their food is often inedible and served in small portions, their lodgings are cramped, and some of the teachers are extremely cruel. Although Jane is adjusting to the change in surroundings, she is still taken aback by the conditions of the school, particularly the food, and the fact that the Reed family did not pay anything to maintain her keep. Bronte hints at the suspicious nature of the school's poor conditions when Helen reveals that "benevolent-minded ladies and gentlemen" make up the tuition and that Mr. Brocklehurst is the treasurer of the house.

Another possible surrogate mother figure for Jane arrives in the form of the beautiful Miss Temple. Her name, with its religious overtones, indicates that she is the only teacher at Lowood who truly upholds the Christian ethic. Bronte also introduces Helen as a confidante and friend for Jane, as well as model of another type of Christianity. Jane is already intrigued and even confused by Helen's calm acceptance of her mistreatment at the school and will soon learn much about patience and emotional control from Helen's example.

Summary and Analysis of Volume I, Chapters 6-10

Volume I, Chapter 6 Summary:

On her second day, Jane learns that life at Lowood School is difficult. The meals are hardly large enough to quell Jane's hunger pangs, and the students are forced to sit through unending sermons. Jane becomes more friendly with Helen and observes as Miss Scatcherd continually berates and even whips Helen, who never makes any response. Helen tells Jane about her personal doctrine of endurance, since the Bible "'bids us return good for evil.'" She also refuses to call Miss Scatcherd cruel; she believes that she has numerous character flaws that Miss Scatcherd is correct to point out. Although Helen is very fond of Miss Temple and finds that she learns more from her, Helen tells Jane that Miss Temple's mild-mannered teaching style does not force her to be actively good; rather, Helen is only passively good, and she believes "'there is no merit in such goodness.'" Jane disagrees with Helen's philosophy; she believes that one should repay goodness with goodness and cruelty with cruelty. She tells Helen about the Reed family, but Helen insists in a long speech that one must forgive one's enemies.

Analysis:

Helen presents her Christian philosophy of forgiveness and endurance: one must bear the sins of others, turn the other cheek, and love thy enemy. Jane, of course, is at odds with this idea, believing that standing up for herself often means fighting back. We have already witnessed several situations in which Jane availed herself of these tactics, particularly the fight against John and her lashing out at Mrs. Reed. The former led to her imprisonment in the red-room, while the latter was a short-lived victory that soon turned into remorse. While Helen's form of Christianity is not useful for Jane, neither is Jane's attitude of self-defense; she must find and develop her own brand of spirituality.

Volume I, Chapter 7 Summary:

Jane passes a difficult first quarter at Lowood, with both the snowy weather and strict environment contributing to her misery. After a long absence from the school, Mr. Brocklehurst visits Miss Temple's classroom and instructs her not to indulge the girls in the slightest way; their privations will remind them of the Christian ethic. He spots a girl with curly hair and deems it unacceptable for an evangelical environment, as are all the top-knots on the girls' heads. Jane, nervous that Mr. Brocklehurst will convey Mrs. Reed's warnings about her behavior to Miss Temple, accidentally drops her slate. Mr. Brocklehurst chastises her in front of the class and three visiting fashionable ladies (Mr. Brocklehurst's family) and tells everyone that she is a wicked liar. He orders Jane to stand on a stool in front of the class to repent for her wickedness and forbids any of the other students from talking to her. Jane's only solace during the day is when Helen disobeys Mr. Brocklehurst's orders and secretly smiles at her.

Analysis:

Jane attempts to test Helen's philosophy of Christian forgiveness when Mr. Brocklehurst punishes her. For the first time in her life, she does not fight back when she is mistreatment and accepts her humiliating punishment of standing on the stool. Yet, Jane inwardly seethes at the injustice and thinks, "I was no Helen Burns." Still, Helen's encouraging smile gives Jane strength, and she feels less isolated even in her despair.

At this point in the text, Bronte points out that Mr. Brocklehurst's version of Christianity is made up of increasingly hypocritical flaws. Though he claims that privation leads to purity, his relatives are dressed in luxurious silks and furs, elegant ensembles that are in clear contrast to the tattered pinafores worn by the students at the school. Mr. Brocklehurst even wants to cut off one girl's naturally curly hair, simply because the curls seem to be an exhibition of vanity. His lust for absolute power over others reveals his truly unchristian nature and also speaks to the male dominated society of the time that provides him with a superior position to the benevolent Miss Temple.

Volume I, Chapter 8 Summary:

When school is dismissed, Jane falls to the floor, filled with self-pity and shame that all of the students despise her because of Mr. Brocklehurst's false accusations. Helen assures her that everyone actually sympathize with her maltreatment. Jane tells Helen of her aching need to have love from others to survive, but Helen tells her that she puts too much stock in love from others; the rewards of spirituality and the glorious afterlife should be our ballast. Miss Temple finds them and takes Helen and Jane to her room, where she asks Jane to tell her version of the story concerning Mrs. Reed. Jane does, strongly insisting upon her innocence, and also mentions Mr. Lloyd's visit to her during her illness. Miss Temple believes her and promises to write Mr. Lloyd for corroboration; when he does, Jane's name will be cleared. She treats the girls to tea and cake and discusses intellectual matters with Helen.

The bedtime bell breaks the heavenly atmosphere, and Miss Scatcherd reprimands Helen for messiness as soon as the girls enter their bedroom. The next day Helen must wear the word "Slattern" on a paper crown around her forehead; at the end of the day, Jane tears it off for her and burns it. A week later Miss Temple announces to the school that Jane's name has been cleared of all of Mr. Brocklehurst's charges, and she is officially reaccepted into the community. Jane is relieved to be cleared of blame and works harder in class, particularly in French and drawing. Despite its failings, Lowood is beginning to grow on her.

Analysis:

In this chapter, Jane reveals her constant need for love and affirmation from others. No doubt a result of her lonely and loveless time at Gateshead, Jane believes that love is the only thing that can make her happy. Helen counters by describing her belief that spirituality is enough; love in the earthly realm is nothing when compared to the spiritual love of God. While it is clear that Jane will never accept these notions completely, Helen is correct in noting that Jane needs to be less reliant on others. In order to gain independence and strength of character, Jane must learn to be dependent on herself and rely less on the love of those around her.

As we have seen before, Bronte uses ice as a motif for cruel, negative destruction, and fire fans out as a symbol of goodness and creation. The fire in Miss Temple's room warms the girls, as does Miss Temple's kindness, conversation, and cake. More interestingly, Jane burns Helen's shameful "Slattern" crown in fire; even when destructive, fire can serve a sort of positive destruction that obliterates evil in the world. This idea of destructive fire as a positive source will reappear in the actions of Bertha Mason later in the text.

Volume I, Chapter 9 Summary:

As spring arrives, Lowood becomes a more pleasant place. However, the warmer temperatures and dampness of the neighboring forest are ideal for breeding disease, and more than half the girls at the school fall ill with typhus. The disease is particularly bad because of the neglectful care that the students receive at the school. Jane, one of the healthy students, enjoys the outdoors, all the more so because Mr. Brocklehurst no longer visits the school. Jane is shocked to learn that Helen is dying, not of typhus, but of consumption. She is not allowed to visit Helen in Miss Temple's room, but Jane sneaks in at night, hoping for one last conversation. Helen accepts her impending death and place in heaven, and tells Jane not to grieve for her; she is happy to be entering heaven. Jane falls asleep in her arms, and Helen dies during the night. Her grave is unmarked at first, but fifteen years later, a marble tablet is placed over it inscribed with the Latin word "Resurgam," or "I will rise again."

Analysis:

Helen maintains her Christian beliefs to the moment of her death, and she fulfills her representation as a Christ figure for Jane, dying so that Jane can learn more of what it means to be a Christian. Although Jane's devotion to Helen is moving, she continues to question Helen's unshakable faith; she wonders, though does not speak aloud, if heaven truly does exist. Although Jane is not willing to accept fully everything that Helen espouses, the "Resurgam" tablet on Helen's grave (placed by Jane, it seems) indicates that she has adapted Helen's beliefs to her own ideology.

Volume I, Chapter 10 Summary:

The epidemic of typhus fever incites an investigation into Lowood's unhealthy conditions and Mr. Brocklehurst's management of the school, and a new group of overseers takes control of the school. With Mr. Brocklehurst's dishonor, the quality of the school improves immensely, and Jane and the other students are able to focus on their education. Jane excels as a student under Miss Temple's guidance for six years and then works as a teacher for an additional two years. When Miss Temple marries and leaves Lowood, Jane is left feeling empty and searching for a "new servitude," a new job serving someone else. She places a newspaper advertisement in search of a post as governess and gains employment for a Mrs. Fairfax at Thornfield Manor. Before Jane leaves to take up this position, she is overjoyed by a visit from Bessie, who is now married to the coachman, Robert Leaven. Bessie brings news of the Reed family, informing Jane that John had become a compulsive gambler and alcoholic while Georgiana had attempted to elope with a certain Lord Edwin Vere but had been foiled by Eliza's intervention. Bessie also mentions that Mr. John Eyre, Jane's uncle, had come to Gateshead seven years ago in an effort to contact Jane before sailing to Madeira to work as a wine-merchant. After the brief visit, Bessie and Jane part ways, and Jane begins her adventure at Thornfield Manor.

Analysis:

This brief transitional chapter spans eight years of Jane's life, during which she matures from an angry girl bent on self-survival into a self-reliant young woman seeking to serve others. Bronte incorporates appropriate endings for some of the more significant characters at Lowood School: Mr. Brocklehurst is removed from power at the school, a just punishment for his negligence and cruelty, while the lovely Miss Temple escapes the difficult life of a teacher and becomes a happily-married woman. Bronte also uses this chapter to incorporate certain narrative details that will be important to the overall plot of the novel. The problems of the Reed family, particularly John's descent into debauchery and vice, foreshadow Mrs. Reed's final confrontation with Jane, as well as hinting that the Reed family is being punished for their mistreatment of Jane. The mention of Mr. Eyre's visit to Gateshead also suggests that he will reappear in some form later on, perhaps with a more important role.

Summary and Analysis of Volume I, Chapters 11-15

Volume I, Chapter 11 Summary:

As Jane arrives in Millcote, she is overcome with anxiety; there is no one at the station to meet her, and she fears that this Mrs. Fairfax will prove to be a second Mrs. Reed. By the time the servant arrives to take her to Thornfield, night has fallen, and Jane can see nothing of the exterior of the house or its grounds. Jane's feels are allayed, however, when she is shown into a cozy room where the elderly Mrs. Fairfax is waiting for her. At first, Jane assumes that Mrs. Fairfax is the owner of the manor, but she soon learns that Mrs. Fairfax is only the housekeeper. Because Mr. Rochester, the manor's owner, is a "peculiar" man who frequently travels on business, Mrs. Fairfax manages the household and estate and thus, responded to Jane's advertisement in the newspaper herself. Mr. Rochester's ward, Adèle Varens, will be Jane's sole pupil at Thornfield. After the initial introduction, Mrs. Fairfax shows Jane to her room, and Jane sleeps peacefully, content to have embarked on a new adventure. The next day, Jane explores the grounds of Thornfield and meets the young Adèle, a garrulous but sweet French girl who chatters in a mixture of French and English. While exploring the house with Mrs. Fairfax, Jane hears a loud, odd laugh. Mrs. Fairfax brushes off the laugh and explains that it was probably one of the servants. She then chastises Grace Poole, a seamstress employed in the house, for "'Too much noise,'" and bids her to "'Remember directions!'"

Analysis:

The introductory chapter to Thornfield plants a few narrative seeds. First, there is an obvious correspondence between Jane and Adèle, both orphans, although Adèle's living conditions are far better. Rochester's background is mysterious, made more so by Adèle's belief that he "'has not kept his word'" to her by constantly abandoning her on his business trips and Mrs. Fairfax's opaque label that he is "'peculiar.'" The ghostly laugh at the end of the chapter, emanating near the attic of the manor, heightens the Gothic suspense of the novel, as do Mrs. Fairfax's curious commands to Grace Poole. Still, despite some strange aspects of Thornfield Manor, Jane feels a certain calm contentment. Not only is she no longer an inferior relative in Gateshead, she is also not a poor student at Lowood. Thornfield provides Jane with the first real opportunity to start her life anew, exploring her independence, maturity, and important position at Thornfield Manor.

Volume I, Chapter 12 Summary:

Life at Thornfield proves to be pleasant, and Jane is pleased with Adèle. Although the girl is somewhat spoiled, Jane recognizes that she is an affectionate and able student and hopes that she will be able to separate Adèle from some of her French affectation. Still, when Jane walks around the attic of Thornfield, she yearns for more experience in the world. Her existence at Thornfield is stable, but her passionate nature still longs for more adventure and passion in her life. During her time near the attic, Jane also frequently hears Grace's bizarre laugh and "eccentric murmurs" and observes other strange behavior. One day in January, Jane walks to town in order to deliver a letter for Mrs. Fairfax and inadvertently startles a gentleman riding on horseback with his dog accompanying him. The gentleman falls from his steed and sprains his ankle, and Jane must help him back on his horse. Although he is unwilling to accept her help, Jane insists, realizing that she never would have been able to be so bold if the rider had been a handsome, young man.

The man asks Jane several questions about Rochester and then departs. When Jane returns to Thornfield, she recognizes the same dog – Pilot – lying on the rug. She asks a servant for an explanation and discovers that it is, indeed, the dog from the road, and Mr. Rochester has just sprained his ankle while riding his horse.

Analysis:

Jane's desire for experience apart from stereotypical female experience is explained in a lengthy passage: "It is narrow-minded in their more privileged fellow-creatures [men] to say that [women] ought to confine themselves to making pudding and knitting stockings, to playing on the piano and embroidering bags." She goes on, and the conflict is clear; Jane desires a life of action and independence that is unavailable to her as a woman during the Victorian time. Jane's thirst for adventure also reveals her passionate nature; although her time at Lowood has taught her to control her emotions beneath a calm exterior, the fiery and passionate Jane Eyre from her childhood at Gateshead still exists and yearns to escape a life of passivity.

In this chapter, Jane also meets Mr. Rochester for the first time. He is instantly cloaked in mystery by his refusal to identify himself to her when they meet along the road. In fact, it is only through the dog that Jane is able to assign an identity to the master of Thornfield Manor. Still, Jane asserts some power at the beginning of their relationship, since Rochester is placed in a weakened position because of his sprained ankle and is reliant on Jane for aid. Another physical impediment forcing Rochester's dependence on Jane will arise later in the novel.

Volume I, Chapter 13 Summary:

With Mr. Rochester home, Thornfield becomes a noisier, busier place, much to Jane's liking. He invites Jane and Adèle to have tea with him and Mrs. Fairfax. Adèle immediately asks if he has a gift for Jane; Jane asserts that the best gift that he can give her is praise of Adele's progress. Mr. Rochester coldly interrogates her about her background but demonstrates more warmth when he looks at Jane's watercolor sketches. After the meal, Jane and Mrs. Fairfax discuss Mr. Rochester. His older brother died nine years ago, whereupon Mr. Rochester inherited the estate, though he avoids the place as much as possible. Mrs. Fairfax's justification that Mr. Rochester finds the place "gloomy" does not satisfy Jane, and Mrs. Fairfax is evasive about

Rochester's other "family troubles."

Analysis:

The mystery concerning Mr. Rochester deepens, and this constitutes the major dramatic thrust of the novel. Gothic novels usually have a romantic component that revolves around passionate, unrequited love; as a stereotypical Byronic hero with a dark, brooding nature and secretive past, Mr. Rochester is an ideal candidate for such a love.

Part of Jane's struggle with Mr. Rochester over the course of the novel will be the assertion of her independence and equality. As we can already see, Rochester only begrudgingly admits Jane's positive qualities, criticizing her even when praising her watercolors. Nevertheless, he demonstrates an obvious interest in her and seems to appreciate her intellectual. As Jane continues to grow in terms of self-reliance and begins to develop feelings for Mr. Rochester, she will undergo a constant struggle between her position as Mr. Rochester's servant and her desire to be something more.

Volume I, Chapter 14 Summary:

During the next few days, Jane sees little of Mr. Rochester as he deals with business and acquaintances. His moods shift rapidly, but Jane cannot figure out their source. One night, during one of his warmer moods, Mr. Rochester gives Adèle her long-awaited gift and is more genial while talking with Jane. Jane keeps scrutinizing his face, a fact he notes; he asks if she finds him handsome, but she gives the honest answer: "No, sir." Mr. Rochester seems to be amused by Jane's answer, and she concludes that he must be slightly drunk. Although the conversation continues, Jane begins to feel increasingly awkward because of Mr. Rochester's position of superiority as her master. Mr. Rochester claims that their relationship should not be one of servitude. Moreover, he does not mean to condescend to her, but his air of superiority comes from his being much older and more experienced. Jane disagrees, arguing that age and experience should automatically confer authority. The conversation moves to the topic of sin and redemption, and Mr. Rochester promises to explain more about Adèle's mother in the future.

Analysis:

Regardless of what Mr. Rochester says about his superiority in regards to experience with Jane, it is clear from his lengthy, involved discussion with her that he views her as his intellectual equal. Though she has a fraction of his worldly experience, Jane acquits herself well with the complicated topics Mr. Rochester brings up and even earns his approval at points for her thoughts. Their flirtation also unofficially begins, as Jane admits to herself that though "most people would have thought him an ugly man," he carries himself with a charismatic, detached confidence.

However, despite his assertion that their relationship is not one in which she is the servant, Mr. Rochester cannot change the social expectations of the time period. Even with their intellectual equality, Jane remains Mr. Rochester's inferior, first as the governess to his ward, but primarily because she is a woman. Still, Mr. Rochester's social domination over Jane will be far more pleasant and affectionate than the submissive position that she assumed with Mr. Brocklehurst or will take up with St. John Rivers at a later point in the novel.

Volume I, Chapter 15 Summary:

One afternoon, while Adèle plays elsewhere, Mr. Rochester takes the opportunity to fulfill his promise to Jane and explain his relationship to Adèle. He was once passionately devoted to her mother, a French opera-dancer named Céline Varens, and despite her superior beauty, she seemed to return his ardor. He spent a fortune treating her to a luxurious lifestyle in Paris until he discovered that he was being cuckolded in a rather humiliating fashion. Mr. Rochester shot the other man in his arm and ended his relationship with Céline, believing that he was entirely done with the affair. However, Céline claimed that the six-month-old Adèle was his daughter and then abandoned her a few years later so that she could run off with an Italian musician. Mr. Rochester was certain that the child was not his, but took responsibility for Adèle anyway and brought her to live as his ward at Thornfield.

Mr. Rochester expects that Jane will be appalled at the prospect of tutoring an illegitimate child, but Jane actually has more sympathy and affection for Adèle after learning of her background. As for Mr. Rochester, these revelations and his confidence in Jane make him seem handsomer and more amiable to her, and she is worried that he will soon leave Thornfield, as Mrs. Fairfax says he always does. That night, as Jane lays awake thinking about everything that Mr. Rochester has told her, she thinks the she hears movement outside her door, then hears a "demoniac" laugh. When she leaves her bedroom, she finds a candle burning in the hallway, sees that Mr. Rochester's door is open, and finds his curtains on fire. He is stupefied by the smoky air, but she wakes him by extinguishing the flames and dousing him with water. She relates what she knows, and he goes into the attic. He returns a few minutes later and says the cause of the fire was Grace Poole, as Jane suspected from the laugh. Mr. Rochester tells her not to speak about the matter to anyone, and then thanks her sincerely for saving his life; he is reluctant for her to leave him. Jane is unable to sleep that night, thinking instead pleasurably of the "hills of Beulah" which, unfortunately, she is not able to reach.

Analysis:

This extended discussion about Céline Varens reveals more of Mr. Rochester's inner character and personality. Significantly, it is this description of Mr. Rochester's flaws that make him seem more attractive to Jane; the jealous anger and desire that he describes mirror Jane's passionate interior and are a welcome contrast from Mr. Brocklehurst's evangelical purity. Even though the discussion of a mistress and an illegitimate child would be deemed inappropriate for a young woman during the time, Mr. Rochester's confidence in Jane heightens the sense of their intellectual (and growing emotional) equality. The fact that Adèle is essentially an orphan is also particularly appealing to Jane; she hopes to take on the same role as surrogate mother that Bessie and Miss Temple had performed for her.

When Jane douses the fire in Mr. Rochester's bedroom, he is again placed in a position of vulnerability that allows her to seize control and independence in the situation. This is also another example of the positive nature of fire; although the fire is potentially destructive, the incident ultimately brings Mr. Rochester and Jane much closer together. However, Jane still recognizes something mysterious about Mr. Rochester: he is quick to blame Grace Poole for causing the fire, and his desire to pin it on her comes across as disingenuous.

However, there is nothing disingenuous about Mr. Rochester's gratitude for Jane having saved his life, and his reluctance for her to leave tells something about his wounded heart. After his bitter betrayal by Céline, he is yearning for a constant love based on more than mere physical attraction, and Jane seems to provide that. Interestingly, when Jane is unable to sleep after saving Mr. Rochester, she is preoccupied by the hills of "Beulah," a term which means "marriage" in Hebrew. Bronte suggests that Jane is already subconsciously thinking of marriage to Mr. Rochester. However, Jane still feels that there is a "counteracting breeze" that would make such a union impossible.

Summary and Analysis of Volume II, Chapters 1-5

Volume II, Chapter 1 Summary:

The day after the fire in Mr. Rochester's bedroom, Jane is shocked to find Grace, who had presumably tried to murder Mr. Rochester, mending the curtains. Grace tells Jane that Rochester fell asleep while his candle was lit, but he awoke before the fire spread too far. Both Jane and Grace seem to know more than each lets on, and they test the other's story; Jane accordingly changes part of her account. Jane is flummoxed by Grace's version of the event, especially because she shows no sign of guilt for what has occurred. Jane is also confused by Mr. Rochester's desire for her not to tell her side of what happened.

When Jane looks for Mr. Rochester to answer her questions about Grace Poole, she discovers that he has left for a social engagement at someone's estate and will be gone for a week or more. Jane already feels his absence from Thornfield and is distressed when she learns that Mr. Rochester is quite a favorite of the ladies he is visiting, particularly the young and beautiful Blanche Ingram. Jane feels foolish for having thought that a plain, poor governess such as herself could ever be of interest to Mr. Rochester. In order to suppress any further romantic inclinations and remind herself of her position in life, she sketches an ugly portrait of herself and then compares it to a gorgeous picture of what she imagines Miss Ingram looks like.

Analysis:

The chapter is split into two sections: the plot developments surrounding the fire, and Jane's preoccupation with Mr. Rochester. After her odd conversation with Grace, Jane realizes that Grace is probably not the culprit of the fire. Not only does she demonstrate little guilt or remorse for her behavior, Mr. Rochester did not even have her removed from Thornfield. Yet, Jane is still not able to figure out the mystery of Grace Poole's presence on the estate. Her only conclusion is that Grace is somehow involved with the fire but is also under direct orders from Mr. Rochester not to reveal her role.

Jane's attempts to find Mr. Rochester and clear up the mystery about Grace lead to the introduction of Blanche Ingram as a character. Jane's sense of inadequacy compared to Blanche Ingram pivots around appearance but also has to do with class. Though Mr. Rochester is not handsome, his high position in society and noble manners determine that his wife must be of an equally high station. Jane's personality, for all its sparkle, cannot make up for her relative poverty and plainness, especially when compared to the beautiful Miss Ingram.

Volume II, Chapter 2 Summary:

Jane is concerned that Mr. Rochester will leave for Europe without returning to Thornfield, something that Mrs. Fairfax acknowledges that he frequently does. However, Jane's fears are allayed when Mr. Rochester sends word that he will be returning to Thornfield in a few days with guests. The servants busily prepare the house for his arrival, and Jane takes the opportunity to observe Grace Poole. She notices that Grace spends nearly all her time on the third-floor and also overhears the servants discussing Grace's high salary and difficult job

Mr. Rochester finally arrives in the company of Miss Ingram and several other men and women. Jane and Adèle keep out of their way as they socialize and dine, and Jane feels particularly out of place among the elegance and sophistication of the visitors. She also notices with increasing dismay that Mr. Rochester appears to prefer the company of Miss Ingram to that of the other ladies. That night, Mr. Rochester invites Jane and Adèle to socialize with the guests after dinner. Jane observes the scene from a distance, paying special attention to Miss Ingram, as Adèle charms the crowd. Miss Ingram and the others speak dismissively of Jane and governesses in general. Miss Ingram goes on to criticize male vanity; beauty should be the domain solely of women, and her future husband will not be her aesthetic equal. She then plays piano, commanding Mr. Rochester to sing. He does, beautifully, and Jane leaves inconspicuously. Rochester meets her outside and beseeches her to return, as she seems "depressed," but Jane declines and turns away before he can see the tears in her eyes. Although he finally allows her to leave, Mr. Rochester informs her that she must come into the drawing room to socialize with the guests every night. He then bids her goodnight, nearly using a term of endearment before stopping himself.

Analysis:

Although Miss Ingram's beauty and confident manner take center stage in the drawing room, the attraction between Mr. Rochester and Jane is evident, especially in his parting words to her. Mr. Rochester cannot help but notice Jane's distress, but he perhaps does not realize that it is because of his attention to Miss Ingram. Similarly, Jane seems to be unwilling to accept the fact that Mr. Rochester nearly said "Good-night, my love." Jane's biggest obstacle to Mr. Rochester remains her own insecurity about her social position and class. Mr. Rochester seems to have feelings for Jane, it is still unclear if he will ever be able to act on them.

Miss Ingram demonstrates the snobbery and classism that strikes at the heart of Jane's curious position that she holds both at Thornfield and previously at Gateshead: poverty in the midst of great wealth. The flip comments of the society ladies about their governesses - and their casual ignorance of Jane in the room - make Jane a virtual prisoner of her social standing. Miss Ingram's lack of intelligence and personal cruelty are particularly upsetting to Jane because she believes that Mr. Rochester deserves better.

This chapter also continues with the mystery of Grace Poole and the third-story attic. Although Jane accumulates some additional clues about Grace's presence at

Thornfield, she is still largely ignorant of the role that Grace plays. Yet, she begins to think of Grace with some pity because of her constant presence on the third floor: she is “as companionless as a prisoner in his dungeon.” "Prisoner" is a loaded word, suggesting imprisonment far beyond physical confines. However, the mysterious events and hints surrounding Grace suggest that she may not be companionless, after all.

Volume II, Chapter 3 Summary:

The guests stay for several stays, and Thornfield becomes a fun and vibrant place. One night the group plays charades; Mr. Rochester pairs off with Miss Ingram, while Miss Ingram's mother says that Jane "looks too stupid" to play. Mr. Rochester and Miss Ingram pantomime a marriage ceremony, among other scenes, until one of the gentlemen solves the charade: Bridewell (a London prison). Jane watches the two of them flirt after their mutual success and is unable to still her growing love for Rochester. However, she realizes that she is not jealous of Miss Ingram, whom she views as disingenuous, dim, and rude, and she hopes that Mr. Rochester will resist Miss Ingram’s attempts to woo him. Rochester's desire to marry for social connections surprises Jane, though she does not hold it against him.

One day while Mr. Rochester is out on business, a handsome man named Richard Mason arrives looking for Mr. Rochester, whom he knows from the West Indies. While he waits for Mr. Rochester’s return, Mason joins the party. That night a gypsy fortune-teller comes to Thornfield; after much debate, the visitors allow her to tell the fortunes of the young ladies in private. Miss Ingram is first and promptly dismisses the teller as a charlatan after returning to the room. Jane notices that she seems upset and suspects that Miss Ingram is disturbed by whatever her fortune was. The three other young ladies have their fortunes told, and report, with glee, that the woman seemed to know everything about them. The fortune-teller insists that she will not leave until she has read Jane's fortune.

Analysis:

The marriage pantomime has obvious parallels to Jane's romantic anxieties. While she cannot believe that Mr. Rochester could prefer the vapid Miss Ingram to her, she does believe that he must marry someone of Miss Ingram's elevated social position. After careful observation of the pair, Jane concludes that the pair will never love each other, but is uncertain that a marriage will not take place nonetheless. Jane is no bride, but a "Bridewell," imprisoned by her social class and confined to limited romantic possibilities.

The arrival of Richard Mason is significant for the plot as another clue to the mystery of the demonic laugh in the third-story attic. Bronte also gives Jane an opportunity to demonstrate her good sense and morality with Mason’s introduction: although Mason is technically a very handsome man, Jane automatically dislikes him, a sentiment that foreshadows his later role in the novel. Bronte also perpetuates the

Gothic theme of the novel by introducing the gypsy fortune-teller. She creates suspense both by ending the chapter on a cliffhanger - what will Jane's fortune reveal? - and by not revealing the nature of Miss Ingram's disturbing fortune.

Volume II, Chapter 4 Summary:

Jane joins the fortune-teller in the library. Although she is initially skeptical of the old woman, Jane becomes entranced by the gypsy's words. The fortune-teller, who admits she has an inside source in Grace Poole, tells Jane several truths, focusing on her feelings toward Mr. Rochester. The fortune-teller predicts that Mr. Rochester will marry Miss Ingram; her previous implication to Miss Ingram that she wants Mr. Rochester only for his money is what disturbed the young lady. She then gives Jane her own fortune, which revolves around Jane's power of reasoning over her emotions.

Suddenly, the old woman reveals her disguise: it is none other than Mr. Rochester. Jane, who had suspected something was amiss from the start, that perhaps the woman was Grace in disguise, is not too upset. When she tells him that Mason has come to Thornfield, Mr. Rochester is shocked and nearly faints. He asks Jane to go into the dining-room and find out what Mason is doing. She reports that the party, Mason included, is socializing. Mr. Rochester, after assuring himself of Jane's loyalty, asks her to whisper an invitation to Mason to see him. She does so, and goes up to bed; late at night she hears Mr. Rochester cheerfully show Mason to his room.

Analysis:

The Gothic element of fortune-teller mingles with the novel's Gothic romance once Mr. Rochester reveals his disguise; mysticism and the supernatural give way to Mr. Rochester's burgeoning love for Jane. The reader is also delighted to see that he is well aware of Miss Ingram's mercenary designs on his estate. Rochester's ability to disguise himself also speaks of his hidden, secretive identity. The disguise of the gypsy is also significant in the way that it plays with inequalities of social class. Not only is Mr. Rochester no longer superior to Jane when he is disguised as the gypsy, he becomes her inferior in class and social position and is barely able to gain access to Thornfield Manor.

In a novel that otherwise focuses on Jane's internal world, Brontë keeps the action moving by constantly introducing new pieces of the mystery of Mr. Rochester's past. Mason's arrival seems innocent, but Jane is unable to shake ominous feelings about him. Moreover, he admits that he is a friend from Mr. Rochester's past, something that even Jane still knows very little about. As if paralleling Jane's uncertainty about the unexpected visitor, Mr. Rochester's feelings concerning Mason change from anxiety to happiness without any explanation. Still, Mr. Rochester's insistence of Jane's loyalty suggests that his seeming ease around Mason later in the evening is only another disguise.

Volume II, Chapter 5 Summary:

During the night, Jane hears a shrill cry from the third story, then someone shouting for Mr. Rochester's help. Jane hears the sounds of someone opening a door and running upstairs. Jane leaves her room, as has everyone else. Mr. Rochester descends from the third story and reassures everyone that a servant has merely had a nightmare. Everyone retires to bed, but Jane goes back and dresses. She thinks she is the only one who heard the words after the scream and is certain that Mr. Rochester's story is false.

After Jane waits for an hour in her room for another sound, Mr. Rochester knocks on her door and asks her to come quietly with him upstairs. He has her bring a sponge and some smelling salts, and then shows her the tapestry-room Mrs. Fairfax had once shown her. He opens a door hidden behind the tapestry, from which again emanates the curious laughter Jane sometimes hears, speaks with whomever is inside, and then emerges and closes the door. Rochester then shows Jane what he has brought her up for: a dazed Mason lies on a chair in the tapestry-room, soaked in blood. Mr. Rochester promises him that Jane will care for him while he fetches the surgeon. He then orders Jane to tend to Mason without any conversation between the two.

Jane is frightened by the baffling circumstances, especially by the thought of Grace in the next room. After two hours, Mr. Rochester returns with a surgeon, Carter, and begins a confusing conversation with Mason. Mason says that "she" bit him when "Rochester got the knife from her," while Mr. Rochester blames Mason for going to see "her" without him; had he waited until tomorrow, Mr. Rochester would have accompanied him. After Carter completes his work, Jane and Mr. Rochester help Mason into a carriage waiting outside. Mr. Rochester instructs Carter to take him home; he will visit in a day or two.

After Mason and Carter leave, Mr. Rochester takes Jane on a walk around the garden. He assures her that neither he nor she is in any danger; the only thing that he has to fear is Mason's saying a certain thing. He asks her to consider the following "hypothetical" situation: a young man made an error - not a crime or an illegal act - that has haunted him forever. No measures he took to deal with it alleviated his misery. He traveled copiously, hoping that would help him, but not until he returned home and met someone new did he feel comforted. He wants to marry this woman, but feels that convention is against him. Is this man, who seeks repentance and salvation in this woman, justified in overturning custom, he asks Jane? Mr. Rochester then admits he is the man and says the woman is - after a long pause - Miss Ingram.

Analysis:

At this point in the novel, it is becoming increasingly difficult for Mr. Rochester to maintain the secret of the third-story attic. Mr. Rochester needs Jane's help after the sudden attack on Mason and, though he is able to take her into his confidence to care for Mason, Mr. Rochester still cannot reveal the truth of what has happened. It is only a matter of time before the truth comes out, but Mr. Rochester exhibits a certain desperation to hide his mystery from Jane for as long as possible.

Significantly, the source of the attack on Mason is female. Although Jane does not know who the woman is (other than possibly Grace Poole), she is both terrified and intrigued by the idea of a female that is uncontrollable by normal social conventions. With her bestial and even carnivorous nature, the mysterious woman in the room seems to have thrown off all of the oppressive ties of the male dominated society.

While Bronte continues to complicate the mystery of Mr. Rochester's past, she also clarifies some of his feelings toward Jane. During his hypothetical story, he is obviously discussing Jane before he changes his position and reveals that Miss Ingram is the object of his desire. Jane describes Mr. Rochester's face as "losing all its softness and gravity, and becoming harsh and sarcastic" when he names Miss Ingram. There is little doubt now that Rochester prefers Jane to Miss Ingram, but there is still an obstacle to the romantic plot. Whoever is in the third-story room - and how it relates to the "error" Rochester committed in his youth - is preventing Rochester's marrying Jane, much more so than the presence of Miss Ingram.

Summary and Analysis of Volume II, Chapters 6-11

Volume II, Chapter 6 Summary:

Robert Leaven, the coachman at Gateshead who is now married to Bessie, visits Jane. He brings news that Jane's cousin, John, has committed suicide. Mrs. Reed has suffered a stroke from shock and is close to death and asking for Jane. Mr. Rochester grants his permission for Jane to leave Thornfield for a week and gives her some money. Jane arrives at Gateshead in the early evening and reunites with Bessie, who tells her that Mrs. Reed is expected to last only another week or two. Jane also talks with Eliza and Georgiana, who are as cold as ever, though their rudeness no longer hurt Jane's feelings. The girls are reluctant to let Jane see their ailing mother, but Jane insists and Bessie arranges a meeting.

Mrs. Reed, her mind clearly elsewhere, does not recognize Jane and speaks harshly of Jane's character. Jane prompts her to discuss her feelings, and Mrs. Reed reveals that she always disliked Jane's mother, her husband's sister, because Mr. Reed always favored her and, subsequently, the orphaned Jane. Mrs. Reed is also under the impression that John is still alive. Jane leaves her bedside.

For ten days Jane does not see Mrs. Reed again, and busies herself with sketching. One day she sketches a portrait of Mr. Rochester that attracts the attention of the Reed girls, whom she also sketches. The episode fosters new intimacy between Jane and Georgiana, who is hung up on her former life in high society London. Eliza maintains her distance from both of them; one night she lashes out at Georgiana for her immaturity and slothfulness, and vows that they will have nothing to do with each other after their mother's death.

Jane visits Mrs. Reed one afternoon while no one is around and reveals her identity. Mrs. Reed apologizes for not bringing her up as one of her own but is still extremely resentful to her because of the late Mr. Reed's preference. Mrs. Reed also gives Jane a letter from her uncle, John Eyre. Mr. Eyre had wanted to adopt Jane and bring him to Madeira with him, but Mrs. Reed had withheld the letter from Jane out of spite. Though Jane offers her forgiveness, Mrs. Reed is unable to let go of her hatred for Jane, and she dies later that night.

Analysis:

The extent of Jane's development over the course of the novel is demonstrated when she returns to Gateshead. Whereas John Reed fell into a dissolute lifestyle of gambling and debauchery, Georgiana became a spoiled debutante, and Eliza became aloof and emotionless, Jane has transformed into a patient and compassionate woman, dedicated to helping others with humility. The initial cold reception from the Reed girls, then, does not disturb Jane as it once might have, nor does Mrs. Reed's unforgiving hatred on her deathbed.

In fact, Jane openly forgives her aunt, telling her that "you have my full and free forgiveness: ask now for God's; and be at peace." Jane seems to have found a third kind of religion, far from the evangelical posturing of Mr. Brocklehurst but still removed from the all-encompassing and self-destructive tolerance of Helen Burns. Jane is forgiving for the past ills done to her by Mrs. Reed; they did not destroy her, but made her stronger. In Jane's version of Christianity, the meek shall not inherit the earth, but neither will the powerful.

In the midst of this emotional chapter, Brontë throws in a twist with the letter from John Eyre. He hints at having accumulated a fortune in Madeira, so Jane's economic status is again complicated. Although she has existed as a poor governess dependent on others for her keeping, perhaps now she has the possibility of achieving personal independence.

Volume II, Chapter 7 Summary:

Jane stays at Gateshead for a month in order to help Georgiana and Eliza. Janc tells us that after her departure, Georgiana moves back to the London and marries a wealthy man, while Eliza enters a convent in France and eventually becomes Mother Superior. Jane returns to Thornfield and is surprised to see Mr. Rochester, who has just returned from London, where he bought a new carriage - most likely to prepare for his wedding. Mr. Rochester is in an infectiously good mood, but Jane worries that he will no longer need her services after his marriage to Miss Ingram. However, the wedding is never mentioned and no preparations are made, and Jane hopes it has been called off.

Analysis:

Jane's time at Gateshead reminds her how important Thornfield and Mr. Rochester have become to her. While Gateshead was her original home, she realizes that now only Thornfield will feel as a home to her, primarily because of her feelings for Mr. Rochester. Jane's interactions with Eliza and Georgiana also remind her how much she has grown over the past nine years. No longer an angry child, resentful of her cruel relatives, Jane is the clear superior in the Reed household and ultimately serves as the peace-keeping mediator between her unhappy cousins.

Upon Jane's return to Thornfield, there are many questions about Mr. Rochester's true intentions with Miss Ingram. Although he purchases a carriage, Mr. Rochester makes no other mention of his impending marriage. Moreover, he refuses to answer any questions about it, and only says that his carriage "will suit Mrs. Rochester exactly." The name could apply to any woman who marries him and, as such, leaves open the possibility that he intends to marry Jane.

Volume II, Chapter 8 Summary:

The summer is glorious at Thornfield, and Jane is happy to be back at her home. One evening Jane runs into Mr. Rochester in the gardens. He reveals that he will marry Miss Ingram in a month and Jane must leave Thornfield; he already has another governess position lined up for her in Ireland. Jane is devastated at the prospect of being so far away from Mr. Rochester, but admits that Miss Ingram's presence will make such a separation necessary.

Mr. Rochester and Jane sit on a bench under a chestnut tree, and Mr. Rochester suddenly changes emotional positions. He tells her that he feels as if they are connected by a cord attached at the heart and asks her to stay at Thornfield. Jane refuses, bringing up the topic of his bride. She also argues that she must mean little to him if he is willing to marry someone so inferior to him as Miss Ingram. Admonishing him for his thoughtless cruelty to her, Jane confesses that she loves him. To her surprise, Mr. Rochester asks her to marry him. At first she believes that he is only mocking her, but he convinces her that he does not love Miss Ingram and could never marry someone who was only interested in his money. After Jane is convinced of his earnestness, she accepts his proposal. Rain forces the overjoyed lovers inside, where they kiss briefly before retiring to their separate quarters. Mrs. Fairfax observes their kiss, but Jane ignores her shocked expression and decides to provide her with an explanation later. That night, a bolt of lightning strikes the tree under which Jane and Mr. Rochester were sitting and splits it in half.

Analysis:

The long build-up to Jane and Rochester's romance culminates in Rochester's marriage proposal, but a greater change comes about within Jane. Oppressed much of her life because of her poverty, she asserts her validity as a person to Rochester, regardless of her material wealth: "Do you think, because I am poor, obscure, plain, and little, I am soulless and heartless? - You think wrong! - I have as much soul as you, - and full as much heart!" The extent of Jane's insecurity is revealed by her inability to believe that Mr. Rochester actually wants to marry her. Although the proposal makes her extremely happy, even Jane wonders about Mr. Rochester's decision to marry someone so beneath his social station.

Jane is also anxious about the prospect of subverting her desires for those of someone else. While her search for love is a driving force in her life, Jane understands that attachment to others comes at a price, and she is not willing to sacrifice her autonomy. A marriage to Mr. Rochester would be one of love and passion, but it might also automatically force her into yet another position of inferiority. Moreover, Bronte will not allow the readers to think that Mr. Rochester's marriage to Jane will proceed without obstacles; when the lightning strikes the chestnut tree, it is hint that the love that Mr. Rochester and Jane share will soon be torn apart.

Volume II, Chapter 9 Summary:

The next morning, Jane is radiant in her love for Mr. Rochester. She feels that she looks prettier, and Mr. Rochester gladly compliments her. He has the wedding for four weeks and tells Jane that he is sending for jewels from London for her to wear. Jane is immediately anxious about the prospect of wearing such ostentation and makes him rescind the order. Mr. Rochester acquiesces but then vows to take her traveling with him around Europe. Once again pledging his love to her, Mr. Rochester finally confesses that he feigned interest in Miss Ingram in order to make Jane jealous.

Jane gets ready to drive to Millcote with Mr. Rochester, and he tells Mrs. Fairfax about their upcoming marriage. Mrs. Fairfax expresses her shock to Jane and warns her to be on her guard, as wealthy men rarely marry their governesses. Jane is hurt by Mrs. Fairfax's insinuations and feels even more unsettled when Mr. Rochester refers to her as Jane Rochester. Adèle wants to go to Millcote with them, and Jane convinces Rochester to bring her along. They ride off, and Rochester jokes to Adèle that he is bringing Jane with him to the moon, and makes a veiled reference to their marriage that Adèle does not understand.

In Millcote, the clothing and jewelry that Mr. Rochester lavishes on Jane embarrasses her. She tells Mr. Rochester that she will not be his "English Céline Varens," but will continue to work as Adèle's governess and maintain her financial independence. She also declines his dinner invitation, though she spends time with him in the evening as he sings and plays piano. He sings a love song and advances toward her, but she refuses to submit to his charms. Jane maintains this distance between them as she falls deeper in love with Mr. Rochester, believing it will serve them better in the weeks before their wedding. Jane also decides to write to her uncle in Madeira, hoping that being John Eyre's heir might make her feel more equal to Mr. Rochester.

Analysis:

Jane already feels somewhat uneasy about her upcoming marriage to Mr. Rochester. Although she loves Mr. Rochester desperately, she is puzzled and hurt by Mrs. Fairfax's disapproval and somehow fears that the wedding will not take place. She also dislikes being dressed in jewels and elegant clothes by Mr. Rochester, feeling as if his presents to her are steadily stripping away her independence. Moreover, Jane wants to ensure that she is not just another mistress in Mr. Rochester's long line of lovers. She also wants to maintain her power over Mr. Rochester as a demonstration of her independence. By rebuffing his passionate advances, Jane is able to hold on to some semblance of control, while simultaneously guaranteeing that she does not become a submissive mistress.

Bronte chooses to highlight Jane's shock at hearing Mr. Rochester call her "Mrs. Rochester." She reminds us that the title of the book is Jane Eyre, and that this name will always define Jane's identity as an independent woman. Interestingly, "Eyre" is a 14th-century word that means "a circuit traveled by an itinerant justice in medieval

England or the court he presided over," and derives from the Old French word "errer," "to travel." If this etymology was Brontë's intention, then the name is ironic. While Jane travels far mentally as she develops into a woman - she is an avid reader, an artist, a musician - her physical journeys are quite circumscribed compared to those of the globe-trotting Mr. Rochester. However, Jane clings to her name, and worries that her independence and perhaps even her identity will be lost when she assumes Mr. Rochester's name.

Volume II, Chapter 10 Summary:

A month passes, and the household has finished preparing for Jane and Mr. Rochester's marriage, which is to take place the following day. Jane is preoccupied for most of the day because of a disturbing incident that occurred during the night. She waits for Mr. Rochester to return from business and tells him about it. While she lay in bed, she seemed to hear a strange howling. She then had a series of dreams revolving around a small child who cries in her arms. Jane woke from her nightmare to see a strange woman in her room. After looking through her closet, the woman found Jane's wedding veil and ripped it in half. The woman then looked at Jane, who fainted.

Mr. Rochester tries to convince Jane that the episode was nothing more than a dream, but she insists that it happened and shows him her wedding veil, ripped in two. Mr. Rochester is horrified and expresses his gratitude that nothing more harmful happened to Jane. He tells her that the woman must have been Grace Poole and promises that he will explain why he keeps her in the house after they have been married for a year and a day. Jane accepts Mr. Rochester's promise, though she is not satisfied with his explanation. Jane sleeps in Adèle's room that night, though she does not fall asleep.

Analysis:

After the previous mysterious incidents at Thornfield, it is clear that the woman who entered Jane's room is related to the laughter from the third story and the fire in Rochester's room (especially because the woman uses a candle as she investigates Jane's closet). It is also clear from the ripped wedding veil that the woman harbors hostility toward the marriage between Mr. Rochester and Jane. However, Mr. Rochester is still unwilling to explain the strange incidents to Jane and continues to use Grace Poole as the scapegoat. Although Jane does not accept his explanations, she realizes that she is unable to force him to divulge secrets about his past.

Jane's nightmares about the crying child speak to her anxiety about leaving her childhood identity of Jane Eyre and ascending to married adulthood as Jane Rochester. The dream could also be read as a bad omen: Jane remembers Bessie telling her that a nightmare about children was a sign of trouble for the dreamer. At this point in the novel, however, Jane is still optimistic about her marriage to Mr. Rochester and hopes that her anxieties will soon dissipate.

Volume II, Chapter 11 Summary:

The next morning, Jane prepares for the marriage ceremony. Instead of wearing the elegant veil that was destroyed by the strange woman, Jane wears a plain veil that she made herself; still, Jane is unable to recognize herself in her wedding dress. She and Mr. Rochester head to the nearby church, but Jane notices that Mr. Rochester looks grim rather that happy about the upcoming ceremony. Jane notices that two strangers enter the church before they do. The priest begins the ceremony, but when he asks Rochester if he will take Jane as his wife, one of the strangers declares an "impediment" to the marriage. The man, Mr. Briggs, introduces himself as a solicitor from London and claims that Mr. Rochester already has a living wife from a previous marriage 15 years ago. Moreover, Briggs asserts that he has a witness to attest to the wife's being alive: Richard Mason. Mason steps forward and reveals that Mr. Rochester's wife was living at Thornfield when he visited three months before, and that he is her brother. Mr. Rochester confesses that the accusation is true, and that his insane wife, Bertha Antoinette Mason, lives in his attic under the careful watch of Grace Poole. He commands that everyone return to the estate to see Bertha and judge for themselves whether or not he was justified in seeking remarriage.

The group goes to Thornfield and up to the third-story attic. In the room where Mason was stabbed and bitten, Grace cooks food while the crazed Bertha runs around like an animal. Bertha lunges at Mr. Rochester and almost strangles him until he ties her to a chair. They all leave the room. Briggs informs Jane that her uncle, John Eyre, is on his sickbed in Madeira but wanted to prevent the marriage, having heard about it from Jane's letter and then from Mason. He suggests that Jane stay in England until she hears more from her uncle. Briggs and Mason leave, and Jane goes into her room alone, reflecting on her sudden change of fortune. All of her hopes have been destroyed, and she no longer knows how she can love Mr. Rochester. She prays to God for help, but is too devastated to even speak the words aloud.

Analysis:

With the revelation of Mr. Rochester's marriage to Bertha, Bronte is able to uncover all of the mysteries of Thornfield and Mr. Rochester's past: the laughter from the third story, Rochester's early error in life and desire for a new wife, Mrs. Fairfax's warning to Jane, the fire in Mr. Rochester's room, and the interloper in Jane's room. Just as Jane has trouble deciding how to judge Rochester, the reader, too, is in a difficult position. Because Mr. Rochester was unaware of Bertha Mason's hereditary madness, he was essentially victimized by the Mason family. Moreover, considering Bertha's propensity for violence, he had little choice but to confine her to the room in the attic, especially when an insane asylum during the time period would have been much more barbaric.

Still, Mr. Rochester would gladly have married Jane despite his preexisting marriage, and Jane would have been diminished to the inferior position of mistress without even realizing it. The biggest difficulty for Jane is that she still loves Mr. Rochester, but her innate sense of right and wrong demand that she cast him aside forever. As evidence of Jane's personal despair, Bronte narrates the bad turn of events with the relentless imagery of ice: "A Christmas frost had come at midsummer; a white December storm had whirled over June; ice glazed the ripe apples..." As in other places in the novel, ice symbolizes destruction, cruelty, hopelessness, and death. In this moment of despair, Jane reaches out to God. While she does not have blind faith in Him (as evidenced by her inability to speak the prayer), God is her last salvation and her last chance (so she believes) to be loved by another.

Summary and Analysis of Volume III, Chapters 1-6

Volume III, Chapter 1 Summary:

After the revelation of Mr. Rochester's previous marriage, Jane returns to her bedroom and wrestles over whether or not she should leave Thornfield. When she leaves her room, Mr. Rochester is waiting for her and earnestly asks for her forgiveness. Jane privately grants it to him, but remains silent. Moreover, she does not allow him to kiss her, as he already has a wife. She begins to feel faint, and Mr. Rochester takes her into the library to recover and apologizes for bringing Jane to Thornfield and for concealing his wife from her. He then proposes that they move to the south of France and live together as man and wife. Adèle will be sent off to school and Grace will remain at Thornfield to watch over Bertha. Jane refuses and begins to cry, saying that though she loves him, she will never be more than a mistress as long as Bertha is alive.

Mr. Rochester explains the conditions surrounding his union to Bertha in order to explain why he does not consider their marriage to be valid. His father left his entire estate to Mr. Rochester's older brother, Rowland, but did not want to leave his second son completely penniless. He sent Mr. Rochester to Jamaica to marry Bertha Mason, the daughter of an old acquaintance, and thus gain her inheritance of 30,000 pounds. Bertha was beautiful and desirable, and although he spent little time alone with her, Mr. Rochester was overwhelmed by her beauty and promptly agreed to the marriage. Soon after the wedding, Mr. Rochester discovered Bertha's mother was in an insane asylum, while her younger brother was a mute idiot. He also realized that his father and brother had been aware of the hereditary madness in the Mason family but had ignored it for the sake of Bertha Mason's vast fortune. Over the four years, Mr. Rochester lived with Bertha in Jamaica and watched her grow increasingly insane, perverse, and violent. In the meantime, Mr. Rochester's father and brother died, leaving him with their fortune. Despairing of his life, Mr. Rochester's contemplated suicide but decided to return to England instead and situated Bertha in the attic cell of Thornfield Manor. Mr. Rochester then traveled the world, searching for a woman to love and being met with disappointment time after time. Finally, he met Jane and instantly knew that she was the one for him.

Jane is torn by Mr. Rochester's confession. She does not want to increase Mr. Rochester's unhappiness, and she doubts that she will ever find anyone who loves her as much as he does. Yet, she realizes that she will always be unhappy with herself if she decides to stay at Thornfield under these circumstances. She kisses Mr. Rochester on the cheek and leaves him, incensed and desperate, in the room alone. That night, Jane dreams that her mother urges her to resist temptation. When she wakes up, she quickly packs her things and leaves Thornfield, all the while resisting the temptation to express her love to Mr. Rochester and stay.

Analysis:

Although Jane's departure from Thornfield is her third major exit from a place after Gateshead and Lowood, it is by far her hardest decision. If she stays, she enjoys the love of a man whom she admits that she worships, as well as the luxury that his wealth affords. However, if she stays and becomes his mistress, she feels that she will lose self-respect. As we have seen throughout the novel, Jane's quest is for self-love and independence as much as it is to attain the love of others. As she puts it to herself, "I care for myself. The more solitary, the more friendless, the more unsustained I am, the more I will respect myself."

Why will marriage destroy Jane's independence? Jane continually uses the excuse of Mr. Rochester's marriage to Bertha, but this is most likely not the true reason; after all, she was at times hesitant about marriage before she learned about Bertha. Rather, we can view Mr. Rochester's marriage to Bertha as a symbol of the inequalities of Victorian marriage, especially in the way it imprisons (literally, in Bertha's case) the female. Jane is worried about similar imprisonment, particularly because of Rochester's higher social standing and the proprietary feelings he has for her (note his frequent pet names for her).

Volume III, Chapter 2 Summary:

Jane remains on the coach for as long as her small supply of money will allow her; she is ultimately forced to get off at the desolate crossroads of Whitcross, ten miles from the nearest town. Finding nature to be her only ally, she heads deep into the heath and seeks protection under a crag. Filled with longing for Mr. Rochester, Jane is unable to sleep. Eventually, she finds comfort in prayer and sees God's presence in the majesty of nature. The next day, Jane sets out on the road in order to find a village. She looks for work, but there is none available, and she is reduced to begging for food.

As night falls, Jane walks toward a lit house in the distance among the marshes. She looks through the windows and sees two young ladies, Diana and Mary, and their elderly servant, Hannah. She listens in on their conversation, and discovers that they are awaiting someone named St. John, and that the ladies' father has recently died. Jane knocks on the door and begs Hannah to let her stay for the night, but Hannah fears that Jane will bring others with her. St. John arrives at the same time and rescues her, bringing her into the house. After being revived with some bread and milk, Jane gives them a false name ("Jane Elliott) but is too exhausted to give any additional details, and says she puts herself in their hands. The members of the household privately discuss the matter, and then put Jane to bed.

Analysis:

After seeking autonomy throughout the novel, Jane finally receives it when she leaves Thornfield. However, she soon learns that truly independent living means sleeping outdoors, scavenging for food, and giving up all dignity. She relies more heavily on God in this chapter than in any others, and, indeed, it is a religious man, St. John, who proves to be her salvation. At the chapter's end, Jane relinquishes whatever independence she had previously claimed: "'I will trust you. If I were a masterless and stray dog, I know that you would not turn me from your hearth tonight: as it is, I really have no fear. Do with me and for me as you like." She willfully succumbs to the identity of a stray dog, putting her faith in others rather than in herself.

Volume III, Chapter 3 Summary:

Jane spends the next three days in bed at the house, attended by Hannah and occasionally seeing Diana and Mary. On the fourth day, Jane gets out of bed and goes downstairs to the kitchen. She assures Hannah that she is not a beggar and discovers that the house is called Marsh End or Moor House, and that the ladies' brother, the parson St. John Rivers, lives in his parish in nearby Morton. Jane reprimands Hannah for passing judgment on her for her poverty, and Hannah apologizes. She then tells Jane the history of Marsh End, which has been in the Rivers family for generations. Although the family used to be wealthy, the late Mr. Rivers lost the family fortune in a business deal, and Diana and Mary were forced to work as governesses to make ends meet. Because of Mr. Rivers' recent death, the ladies have returned to the house for a few weeks.

Diana, Mary, and St. John soon return, and the sisters direct Jane to keep out of the kitchen and sit into the parlor. St. John is there, and Jane examines his classically handsome face. Jane tells them that she has no home or friends and refuses to reveal her last residence. Instead, she provides a bare-bones history of her life, admitting that the name "Jane Elliott" is not her real name. She asks to stay with them until she is able to find work, and St. John promises to find her a job.

Analysis:

Brontë draws an obvious contrast between the altruistic and kindly Rivers children - Diana, Mary, and St. John - and the spoiled and cruel Reed children - Eliza, Georgiana, and the far from holy John. Although she does not reveal Jane's true relationship with the Rivers' siblings, Brontë does provide another model of family and familial connection for Jane to aspire toward.

The fact that St. John is a parson also suggests that Jane's view of religion will undergo further revision in the following chapters. At this point in the text, she is still searching for a model of Christianity that is applicable to her own life; the Christianity of both Mr. Brocklehurst and Helen Burns was incompatible with Jane's passionate nature.

Interestingly, Jane is once again in a financially difficult position, compared to those around her. Whereas before she was consistently a poor figure in a rich environment (in the Reed house and at Thornfield), she is here identified as a beggar. The Rivers siblings are in the midst of financial difficulties themselves, but Jane is still inferior to them in terms of her economic stability. Moreover, although she has indeed been begging, Jane resists this definition, seeking an identity that is divorced from money.

Volume III, Chapter 4 Summary:

Over the next few days, Jane grows closer to Diana and Mary; she is especially drawn to Diana's charisma. St. John, however, remains a detached figure and is generally reserved and brooding on the few occasions that she sees him. However, one day, Jane hears him preach in his church, and his stern Calvinist oration about predestination has a profound, thrilling effect on her, although it leaves her saddened. Despite his eloquence, she feels he has not "found that peace of God which passeth all understanding" anymore than Jane has.

After a month, Diana and Mary prepare to return to their positions as governesses elsewhere in England. St. John plans to shut up the house after his sisters leave, but he is able to offer Jane the position of headmistress for a girls' school he is establishing in Morton. Jane gladly accepts, but St. John suspects that Jane will grow bored of the job and soon leave. Before Mary and Diana leave, St. John tells them that their uncle John is dead. They are relieved by this news, and Diana explains that their father and uncle quarreled, and Mr. Rivers lost most of his fortune while their uncle profited greatly. The uncle has left almost all his 20,000 pounds to an unknown relation, while giving a pittance to the Rivers children. Over the next few days, all of the inhabitants of the house leave.

Analysis:

Jane finds greater intimacy with the residents at Marsh End, especially the two sisters. Significantly, Jane had very few female friends during her life; only Helen Burns and Miss Temple even fall in the category. Although she has left her home at Thornfield, Jane has gained enough self-assurance to become friends with other self-reliant women. The growing friendship between Jane and Diana and Mary also serves as yet another of Brontë's hints about their relationship to Jane. The astute reader will notice some connections between the fortune left by the Rivers's uncle and that of Jane's own uncle John Eyre.

St. John's calculated, somewhat cold Calvinism is not an ideal Christian model for Jane, as she finds in it "a strange bitterness; an absence of consolatory gentleness." While Helen Burns's doctrine of tolerance and forgiveness was too meek for Jane, St. John's is far too intolerant and unforgiving. Still, Jane cannot help but be intrigued by St. John's strikingly handsome face and passionate sermon.

Volume III, Chapter 5 Summary:

Jane is installed in a cottage at Morton and immediately starts teaching as the headmistress of the school. Her students are largely uneducated, but many are eager learners, and Jane resolves to discard her self-pity over her situation and work hard to help her students achieve academic heights. She maintains that her decision was right: she is better off being free and in somewhat difficult conditions than staying with Mr. Rochester as a beloved slave in luxury.

During a brief visit, St. John finally opens up to Jane and tells her that a year ago he was unhappy as a priest and was looking for a more exciting lifestyle. He was close to picking a new career until he heard a call from God to become a missionary. A beautiful, angelic young lady, Rosamond Oliver, interrupts them; her father has told her that St. John's new school has opened, and she wants to know how the first day was. Jane realizes that Miss Oliver is the wealthy benefactress of the school. Miss Oliver invites St. John to visit her father, but he stolidly declines and the two part ways. As she observes St. John's interactions with Miss Oliver, Jane comes to the conclusion that the two are in love.

Analysis:

Jane has come full circle; she was once a neglected, poor orphan at Lowood and is now headmistress of her own school. Following in the mold of the kindly Miss Temple, she resolves to help her students who, while not orphans, are poor and largely uneducated. In fact, Jane nearly turns to snobbishness when describing the students and must remind herself that "these coarsely clad little peasants are of flesh and blood as good as the scions of gentlest genealogy." She admits that she is unhappy in her situation, but Jane continues to rationalize her decision to leave Mr. Rochester as fulfillment of her quest for independence.

Miss Oliver serves as the first example in the novel of someone who is rich, beauty, and good-natured (everyone else has only one or two of the qualities). Jane is quick to realize that St. John and Miss Oliver are in love, but she is unable to see how love fits into St. John's plans to become a missionary.

Volume III, Chapter 6 Summary:

Jane adjusts to the rigors of teaching and eventually finds her students to be able and amiable. She becomes a well-liked fixture in the community and finally feels that she has found a place to prosper. Still, some nights, Jane still dreams being with Mr. Rochester. Miss Oliver frequently visits her, and Jane can see the effect that she has on St. John, who does his best to conceal his feelings; though he clearly desires her, he has devoted himself to his religion. Jane visits her and Mr. Oliver at Vale Hall and learns that Mr. Oliver wants his daughter to marry St. John.

One day, St. John visits while Jane is working on a portrait of Miss Oliver she has been asked to do. He is transfixed by the portrait, and Jane tells him of Miss Oliver's affection for him before boldly suggesting that he marry her. St. John confesses that he loves Miss Oliver but cannot relinquish his calling from God. Miss Oliver may be beautiful, but she would be a terrible missionary, and thus, St. John cannot even consider her to be his wife. Suddenly, St. John notices something on the edge of the portrait's canvas – Jane is not sure what it is - and furtively rips it off and leaves.

Analysis:

St. John is similar to Jane in that he is unwilling to give up his independence for love. Although Miss Oliver loves him, her beauty and higher social status would hamper his quest to be a missionary; he would rather seek his own calling in life than be beholden to someone else, even someone he might love passionately. However, when she discovers St. John's love for Miss Oliver, Jane's first impulse is not to support St. John's decision to reject love, but rather to urge St. John to marry her. She believes that a couple with such passionate love for one another should ultimately be together, a belief that clearly speaks to Jane's subconscious feelings for Mr. Rochester.

Summary and Analysis of Volume III, Chapters 7-12

Volume III, Chapter 7 Summary:

One night in winter, St. John visits Jane at her cottage. He tells her a story of a poor curate who, twenty years ago, fell in love with a rich man's daughter and married her; her friends disowned her after the wedding. They both died within two years, leaving behind a daughter, who was raised by her aunt-in-law, Mrs. Reed of Gateshead. St. John recounts the rest of Jane's life up until her departure from Thornfield, after which everyone searched for her to no avail. Although Jane realizes that St. John is talking about her, she still does not identify herself as "Jane Eyre." St. John informs her that he has just received a letter from Mr. Briggs, in which the solicitor asserts the importance of finding the missing Jane Eyre.

The reason Briggs sought Jane, St. John says, is because Jane's uncle, Mr. John Eyre of Madeira, has died and left her his great fortune of 20,000 pounds. Jane is stunned and reveals her true identity to St. John. Still, she does not understand why Briggs attempted to reach her through St. John. St. John reveals that his full name is St. John Eyre Rivers, and his mother's brother is Jane's uncle. St. John also admits that he tore the scrap of paper from Miss Rosamond's portrait because it was her legal signature and allowed her to corroborate the story. Jane is as overjoyed to discover that she has cousins as she is by the fortune. Jane decides to split the fortune four ways among the cousins and live to at Moor House with Diana and Mary, but St. John urges her to reconsider; the fortune was left solely to her, and she should not feel obliged to share it. Jane refuses to change her decision, asserting that having close relations is more important to her than the money; she also discards the notion of ever marrying. St. John pledges to treat her as his sister, and Jane promises to remain headmistress until he finds a replacement at the Morton school. Eventually, Jane persuades her cousins to share her fortune, and they each inherit 5,000 pounds.

Analysis:

In this chapter, Brontë incorporates various hints scattered throughout the novel – including the existence of Jane's wealthy uncle John Eyre and the scrap of paper St. John tore from Jane's portrait – to finally establish Jane's financial independence. Moreover, Jane finally discovers her real family: coming across her long-lost cousins, purely by accident. Although the fortune is a deus ex machina plot twist that, as Jane says, gives her a victory she "never earned and do[es] not merit," she has, in many ways, earned it. By being selfless, humble, and eschewing the fortune Rochester would have given her in return for her virtual servitude, Jane is most deserving of a gift that will finally give her true independence. This particular plot conclusion is perhaps the most improbably of the plot, but it allows Brontë to overcome several of the difficulties that were obstructing the relationship between Jane and Mr. Rochester.

Volume III, Chapter 8 Summary:

Jane finishes her duties at the school before Christmas and returns to Moor House to prepare for a holiday with her newfound family. Diana and Mary are overjoyed with the changes in their situation, particularly having Jane as their cousin, but St. John seems to be increasingly aloof. They all soon hear that Miss Oliver is to marry the wealthy Mr. Granby. St. John is stoic and claims that he is glad, as it has cleared the way for his mission to India. While Jane loves living with her female cousins, St. John continues to treat Jane coldly, treating her more as a servant than as a relative. He also asks her to postpone her study of German and instead study "Hindustani," the language needed for missionary work in India. Although Jane still feels connected to Mr. Rochester, she notices that St. John is able to influence her more and more with each passing day.

One spring day, St. John asks Jane to go to India with him as a missionary and as his wife. Jane resists, telling him that she will go to India as a missionary but she cannot marry him. St. John insists that Jane has the right qualities for a missionary wife, but Jane continues to refuse. She scorns St. John's conception of marriage since it is one devoid of love, and St. John, in turn, accuses Jane of denying Christianity by refusing to marry him. St. John promises to give Jane two weeks to reconsider his proposal and then leaves the room.

Analysis:

In this chapter, autonomy again appears as Jane's main desire. Though the idea of being a Christian missionary is appealing to her as a way to add structure to her life (and continue her notion of serving others), she is unwilling to be imprisoned in another marriage. While she rejected Mr. Rochester's proposal because she feared a status of inferiority, she refuses St. John's proposal because love would not be a part of it.

Jane thus rejects St. John's model of Christianity, as she formerly rejected Helen Burns's and Brocklehurst's. While St. John's Christianity is neither overly meek nor hypocritical and corrupt, his is emotionless. As Jane said earlier, he has not found his peace with God, and his religious zeal seems more mechanical than human. Although Jane is prepared to deal with questions of morality and duty, she refuses to believe that true Christianity requires individuals to strip themselves of all love.

Volume III, Chapter 9 Summary:

Over the several days, St. John continues to insist that Jane marry him and travel to India as his wife. Although she is upset by his coldness to her, Jane still will not accept his proposal, and St. John rejects the possibility of taking her along as his unmarried assistant. Diana supports Jane's decision, arguing that St. John will only ever treat her as a tool that he can use to achieve his calling to God. Later, St. John is his usual polite and aloof self to Jane while reading from "Revelations," though he insinuates that Jane will end up in Hell for her refusal to marry him. The next morning, he leaves for Cambridge, and in a sincere moment, again tells Jane she should reconsider her decision while he is gone. She is so moved by his warmth and power of speaking that she is tempted to yield to his desires. Just when she is about to accept him, she has a mystical vision and hears Mr. Rochester's voice from a great distance, calling: "Jane! Jane! Jane!" St. John's influence over her is broken, and Jane announces that she is going to seek out Mr. Rochester. In her room alone, she prays and feels rejuvenated.

Analysis:

The debate between Jane's need for autonomy and her desire to succumb to St. John's powers continue, but the outcome is rarely in doubt. Instead, Jane's love for Mr. Rochester deepens, and she now has the tools needed for a liberated marriage: self-esteem, the love of others (including relatives), financial independence, and an identity that she has carved out on her own. While St. John would oppress these traits as he led Jane through his missionary work in India, a marriage to Rochester would no longer squelch these qualities.

With such assurance, Jane can now also turn to religion in a positive, healthy manner, one different from all other models she has observed: "I...prayed in my way - a different way to St. John's, but effective in its own fashion. I seemed to penetrate near a Might Spirit; and my soul rushed out in gratitude at His feet." Jane's spirituality has neither the hypocritical postures of Brocklehurst's evangelism, the meekness of Helen Burns's forgiveness, nor the detachment of St. John's proselytizing, but attains a transcendence of love and connection lacking in the philosophies of those three.

Volume III, Chapter 10 Summary:

The next morning, Jane wonders if she really heard Mr. Rochester's voice calling to her or if she was merely imagining it. She finds a note from St. John requesting her final decision when he returns from Cambridge, but Jane's mind is on Rochester, and she leaves that afternoon for Thornfield. Although only a year has passed, Jane feels as if she has a new identity and anxiously awaits the sight of Mr. Rochester at the Manor. After two days on the couch, Jane arrives, only to find Thornfield in ruins, destroyed by a fire. At a nearby inn, Jane learns what happened: one night Bertha Mason escaped from Grace's watch and set fire to the governess's old bed. Mr. Rochester was able to get all of the servants out of the burning house, and tried to save his wife, but he was too late: Bertha jumped to her death from the roof. Mr. Rochester lost his eyesight and a hand during the fire and has since been relegated to Ferndean, a nearby manor house, staffed by the elderly John and Mary.

Analysis:

While the fire at Thornfield destroyed both Mr. Rochester's estate and his eyesight, fire continues to be a positive force even in its destruction. Bertha Mason was the one remaining obstacle to a marriage between Mr. Rochester and Jane. With her death, Mr. Rochester is finally a free man and has the ability to marry Jane without forcing her to sacrifice her morality. The fire also equalizes the relationship between Jane and Mr. Rochester. While she has recently gained her own fortune, he has lost much of his. Moreover, Mr. Rochester's blindness and lost hand place him in a position of vulnerability in which the social expectations of male domination in marriage no longer exist.

Volume III, Chapter 11 Summary:

Jane travels to the desolate Ferndean and observes Mr. Rochester from a distance. Although his body is unchanged, his face seems so much more tortured and despairing than it was before. Jane knocks on the door, and Mary invites her in. Jane brings a tray to Mr. Rochester, and he eventually realizes who she is. He is overjoyed by her return, and she tells him that she is now independently wealthy and offers to stay with him as his nurse; she contends she does not care about marrying anyone. Mr. Rochester anxiously asks if she is revolted by his blindness and by the loss of one of his hands, but she assures him that she is not and promises never to leave him.

The next day, Jane tells Mr. Rochester of everything that had happened to her in the past year, including St. John's marriage proposal. Mr. Rochester is obviously jealous of St. John, and insists that he would never have treated her as his subjugated mistress, but as his equal. Jane assures him that she does not love her cousin, and that her heart belongs only to Mr. Rochester. He asks her to marry him, and she agrees. As they walk together, finally able to achieve happiness together, Mr. Rochester reveals that four nights before, he had prayed to God for a reunion with Jane and involuntarily recited Jane's name three times. Jane admits that she heard his voice in her own mystical vision that night and answered him in turn.

Analysis:

Jane's search for religion culminates with the mystical union between her and Mr. Rochester. Their bond is based on a profound, spiritual connection that passes through God and is formed by love. Mr. Rochester's spiritual development over the course of the novel also helps to make him a more suitable match for Jane; now he possesses much of the same reverence toward God that Jane had always exhibited. Together in their love, Jane and Mr. Rochester are able to fulfill God's calling while simultaneously attaining their own happiness.

Brontë also takes this opportunity to assert Jane's independence once again. Jane proudly admits to her autonomy, asserting: "I am an independent woman now," but also demonstrates it by a symbolic action at the end of the chapter: "I took that dear hand, held it a moment to my lips, then let it pass round my shoulder: being so much lower of stature than he, I served both for his prop and guide." Though Jane is of "much lower stature" than Rochester - she comes from humbler origins - she now has sufficient strength and independence to lead Rochester and, indeed, he is dependent on her for it. Her quest for autonomy is complete, and it does not exclude a happy marriage to someone she loves.

Volume III, Chapter 12 Summary:

Jane and Rochester have a quiet marriage. She writes to Moor House and Cambridge to tells her cousins the news; Diana and Mary send their joyful congratulations, but St. John never acknowledges her marriage. Finding Adèle unhappy at her strict boarding school, Jane enrolls her in a better school closer to home, and she is able to blossom into a lovely young woman. Jane writes that she is writing this narrative after ten years of marriage to Mr. Rochester, and she is still enthralled with her union to her husband. Their marriage is one of joy and equality, and Jane never faces the inferiority that she feared married life would bring. Two years into their marriage, Mr. Rochester regained vision in one of his eyes and he is able to see their newborn son. Jane also reports that Diana and Mary both married happily, while St. John remained a "faithful servant" to God and became a missionary in India. In his last letter to Jane, St. John reiterates that he has done his duty to God and hopes that the Lord Jesus will come for him soon.

Analysis:

Two major themes - Jane's desire for love and her search for religion - mingle with her greatest preoccupation, her need for independence, in different ways. As we have already seen, she has blended love with independence in her marriage with Rochester: "To be together is for us to be at once as free as in solitude, as gay as in company."

However, Jane is also able to maintain a spiritual relationship with God without sacrificing her independence. St. John, on the other hand, is not, as his letter to Jane reveals: "My Master...has forewarned me. Daily he announces more distinctly, 'Surely I come quickly!' and hour I more eagerly respond, 'Amen; even so come, Lord Jesus!'" Brontë ends the novel on this note to underscore the connections between St. John's religious devotion and her concern with female subjugation. Unlike St. John, Jane fears yielding her will to her "Master" (or husband), and Brontë has used Bertha's imprisonment in the attic and Jane's imprisonment in the red-room as symbols for the ways in which Victorian society can confine women in marriage or in any other regard. Thus, Brontë concludes the novel on a critique of religion while demonstrating that marriage need not incorporate its restrictions of individual will. This ending also serves as a reminder of the importance of love in a relationship with God: St. John believed that love had no play in a life meant for God, and he ultimately dies alone. Jane, on the other hand, is able to combine her love with her religion and achieve all of her heart's desires.

Suggested Essay Questions

1. How does Charlotte Brontë incorporate elements of the Gothic tradition into the novel?

   In the Gothic literary tradition, the narrative structure of a text is meant to evoke a sense of horror or suspense, often through the use of the supernatural, hidden secrets, mysterious characters, and dark passion. Brontë incorporates each of these elements into the novel and especially highlights the importance of the mysterious Byronic hero in the form of Mr. Rochester. Brontë also emphasizes the Gothic nature of Thornfield Hall and incorporates the figure of the Madwoman in the Attic as the primary conflict of the novel. Brontë uses these Gothic elements as a way to heighten the tension and emotion over the course of the narrative, as well as to reveal an almost supernatural connection between Jane and Mr. Rochester.
2. Is Jane Eyre a likable protagonist? Why or why not?

   Jane is an atypical heroine for the Victorian period, and even for contemporary literature, because she is not beautiful in a traditional sense. Unlike Georgiana and Blanche Ingram, who are each lauded as exceptional beauties in the text, Jane is small and slight, with ordinary features and a slightly elvish appearance. With that in mind, Jane is particularly likable protagonist because she is not an idealized figure; her personal and physical faults make her seem more realistic and allow readers to relate to her more closely. At the same time, however, Jane's firm morality and harsh rejection of Mr. Rochester may seem rather cold and unlikable to the more passionate readers. Still, Jane's independent spirit and courage against all obstacles ensure that she is a protagonist to be valued and encouraged.
3. How does Jane Eyre compare to Bertha Mason?

   As the stereotypical Madwoman in the Attic, Bertha is presented as a clear antagonist to Jane in the novel. Not only does she personify the chaos and dark animal sensuality that contrasts so sharply to Jane's calm morality, Bertha is ultimately the sole obstacle between Jane and Mr. Rochester and their eventual happiness. However, while Jane and Bertha seem to be wholly distinct from each other, Bronte does suggest that the two characters have significant similarities. Although Jane is calm and controlled as an adult, she exhibits much of the same passion and bestiality as a child that Bertha displays in her madness. Moreover, though Jane leaves Thornfield rather than become Mr. Rochester's mistress, she still possesses the same qualities of sensuality as Bertha but is simply more successful at suppressing them.
4. How does the novel comment on the position of women in Victorian society?

As a woman, Jane is forced to adhere to the strict expectations of the time period. Thought to be inferior to men physically and mentally, women could only hope to achieve some sort of power through marriage. As a governess, Jane suffers under an even more rigid set of expectations that highlight her lower-class status. With this social construct in mind, Jane has a submissive position to a male character until the very end of the novel. At Lowood, she is subservient to Mr. Brocklehurst; at Moor House, she is under the direct control of St. John Rivers; and even at Thornfield, she is in a perpetually submissive position to Mr. Rochester. Over the course of the narrative, Jane must escape from each of these inferior positions in an effort to gain her own independence from male domination. After her uncle leaves her his fortune, Jane is able to achieve this independence and can marry Mr. Rochester on her own terms, as an equal. Yet, Bronte emphasizes that Jane's sudden inheritance and resulting happy ending are not typical for women during the time period. Under most circumstances, Jane would be forced to maintain a subservient position to men for her entire life, either by continuing her work as a governess or by marrying an oppressive husband.

5. Considering his treatment of Bertha Mason, is Mr. Rochester a sympathetic or unsympathetic character?

   Although Mr. Rochester's treatment of Bertha may seem to be cruel, it is difficult not to feel some sympathy for his situation. Mr. Rochester married Bertha under false pretenses; he was unaware of her hereditary madness and was swept away by her exotic beauty and charm. After discovering his wife's madness, Mr. Rochester does not cast her out but rather attempts to make her life as comfortable as possible. Although Bertha's chamber in Thornfield seems inhumane, it is important to note that the conditions in madhouses of the time period would have been far worse. Mr. Rochester also is more sympathetic when we consider his extreme unhappiness and loneliness: he was fooled by the appearance of love and has been paying for his mistake ever since.

6. How does Mr. Rochester compare to St. John Rivers?

   Throughout the novel, Bronte associates Mr. Rochester with fire and passion and St. John Rivers with ice and cold detachment. Bronte also presents Jane's potential union with each man as profoundly different. With Mr. Rochester, Jane would be forced to sacrifice her morality and sense of duty for the sake of passion. With St. John Rivers, however, Jane would have to sacrifice all sense of passion for the sake of religious duty. Significantly, Bronte also suggests that St. John may not be too different from Mr. Rochester. He is passionately in love with Rosamond Oliver, and his feelings for Rosamond seem to mirror Mr. Rochester's fiery emotions for Jane. However, St. John forces himself to suppress his feelings in favor of a cold evangelical exterior and, as a result, lives his life in solitude.

7. Why is Jane unable to stay with Mr. Rochester after his marriage to Bertha Mason is revealed?

Although Jane is very much in love with Mr. Rochester, she is unable to give in to the passion that she feels. Her eight years at Lowood School and her conversations with Helen Burns taught her the importance of suppressing passion and lust with morality and a sense of duty. If Jane were to stay with Mr. Rochester, it could only be as his mistress, and Jane is unwilling to sacrifice her sense of right and wrong in order to placate her personal desires. However, because Jane's love for Mr. Rochester is so strong, she realizes that she will be unable to resist him and her own desires if she remains at Thornfield Manor. Thus, when Jane leaves Thornfield, she sacrifices her personal happiness in order to save them both from committing a sin that would destroy the purity of their love.

8. What is the significance of Charlotte Brontë ending the novel with a statement from St. John Rivers?

In the last chapter of the novel, Brontë describes Jane's happiness with Mr. Rochester: they have married, had children, and Mr. Rochester has regained sight in one of his eyes. Yet, instead of ending the book on this happy note, Brontë concludes the novel with a letter from St. John in India in which he mentions a premonition of his death. St. John has done his duty to God by working as a missionary in India, but his existence still seems small and lonely in comparison to the joyous life that Jane has made with Mr. Rochester. Brontë suggests that even the most pious life is meaningless if it is devoid of love. St. John has a chance for love with Rosamond Oliver, but he sacrificed his happiness with her because he did not believe that love could co-exist with religion. Jane's ending with Mr. Rochester demonstrates the falsity of St. John's beliefs and reminds the readers of what could have happened to Jane if she had given up her love for Mr. Rochester.

9. What is the role of family in the novel?

The novel traces Jane's development as an independent individual, but it can also be read as a description of her personal journey to find her family. In each of the five stages of the novel, Jane searches for the family that she has never known. At Gateshead, the Reed family is related to her by blood and, while Bessie serves as a sort of surrogate maternal figure, Jane is unable to receive the true love and affection that she desires. At Lowood, Jane finds another maternal figure in the form of Miss Temple, but again, the school does not become a true home to her. When Jane reaches Thornfield and meets Mr. Rochester, she finally finds the love and family for which she has thirsted: Thornfield becomes her home because of her love for Mr. Rochester. However, because of Mr. Rochester's existing marriage to Bertha Mason (a union which nullifies any of Jane's familial connections to the Manor), Jane must move on and attempt to replace the family that she has now lost. Ironically, when Jane stays at Moor House, she actually discovers her true family: the Rivers siblings are her cousins. Yet, Jane's true sense of family remains with the love she feels for Mr. Rochester and, by returning to him at Ferndean and finally accepting his marriage proposal, she is able to fulfill her desire for a true family at last.

10. How does the novel relate to Charlotte Brontë's personal life?

Many aspects of the novel are autobiographical. Lowood School is based on the Clergy Daughters School at Cowan Bridge, where Jane and her sisters studied after their mother's death. Brontë's school has similarly poor conditions, and Brontë modeled Mr. Brocklehurst after the Reverend William Carus Wilson, an evangelical minister who managed the school. Brontë also informed the death of Helen Burns by recalling the deaths of her two sisters during a fever outbreak at their school. John Reed's descent into gambling and alcoholism relates to the struggles of Brontë's brother, Patrick Branwell, during the later years of his life. Most importantly, Jane's experience as a governess were modeled directly on Brontë's own experiences as a governess in wealthy families.

The Madwoman in the Attic: Angel or Monster?

In "Jane Eyre," the character of Bertha Mason serves as an ominous representation of uncontrollable passion and madness. Her dark sensuality and violent nature contrast sharply with Jane's calm morality, and it is no surprise that Bertha's presence at Thornfield is a key factor in transforming Mr. Rochester into a stereotypical Byronic hero. Moreover, Bertha's marriage to Mr. Rochester serves as the primary conflict of the novel, and it is only after her death that Jane is able to achieve personal happiness by marrying Mr. Rochester. However, Bertha's position as the "Madwoman in the Attic" also speaks to larger social questions of femininity and authorship during the Victorian period.

In 1979, Sandra Gilbert and Susan Gubar made a breakthrough in feminist criticism with their work "The Madwoman in the Attic: The Woman Writer and the Nineteenth-Century Literary Imagination." In the 700-page text, Gilbert and Gubar use the figure of Bertha Mason as the so-called "Madwoman in the Attic" to make an argument about perceptions toward female literary characters during the time period. According to Gilbert and Gubar, all female characters in male-authored books can be categorized as either the "angel" or the "monster."

The "angel" character was pure, dispassionate, and submissive; in other words, the ideal female figure in a male-dominated society. Interestingly, the term "angel" stems directly from Coventry Patmore's 1854 poem "The Angel in the House," in which he described his meek and pious wife. In sharp contrast to the "angel" figure, the "monster" female character was sensual, passionate, rebellious, and decidedly uncontrollable: all qualities that caused a great deal of anxiety among men during the Victorian period.

However, Charlotte Brontë (as well as many other contemporary female authors) did not limit her characterizations to this strict dichotomy between monster and angel. Jane Eyre possesses many of the qualities of the so-called angel: she is pure, moral, and controlled in her behavior. Yet, at the same time, she is extremely passionate, independent, and courageous. She refuses to submit to a position of inferiority to the men in her life, even when faced with a choice between love and autonomy, and ultimately triumphs over social expectations. Moreover, Jane's childhood adventures demonstrate much of the same rebelliousness and anger that characterize the "monster." It is clear that Jane's appearance of control is only something that she learned during her time at Lowood School; she still maintains the same fiery spirit that defined her character as a child.

With the character of Bertha Mason, Brontë has a more difficult time when it comes to blending the distinctions between angel and monster. The readers only meet Bertha when she is in the depths of madness, having been confined in the third-story attic of Thornfield for nearly fifteen years, and there is not enough interaction between her and the other characters to demonstrate any "angelic" behavior. Yet, Bertha's position as the obstacle to Jane's happiness with Mr. Rochester, as well as her state of complete imprisonment, suggest that her madness may have been partially manufactured by the male-dominated society that forced her to give up her wealth in marriage to Mr. Rochester. Moreover, the similarities between Bertha's behavior in the third-story attic and Jane's actions as a child in the red-room suggest that neither character is full angel or full monster but rather a combination of the two.

While Brontë does not differentiate between angel and monster in her portrayal of Jane and Bertha, she does, however, argue for moderation of the passions in all of her characters. Mr. Rochester and Bertha both have too much passion in their lives, while St. John Rivers has too little. Bertha's passion manifests as madness, while Mr. Rochester's passion is displayed in his debaucherous behavior on the continent and his determination to make Jane his mistress. St. John, on the other hand, suppresses all of his passion and love for Rosamond Oliver, and thus becomes a cold and aloof man whose only desire is to fulfill his duty to God. Of the three characters, Mr. Rochester is the only one who eventually achieves a balance of passion; after Jane's departure from Thornfield and the loss of his eyesight, he becomes much more spiritual and is able to achieve the same emotional moderation that Jane exhibits throughout the novel.

Although Bertha does serve as one of the seeming villains of the novel, she should be seen more as a critique of a society in which passionate woman are viewed as monsters or madwomen. Charlotte Brontë's act of writing a novel – particularly such a Gothic one - was no doubt equally threatening to the men of her time period. In some ways, Brontë's decision to merge the identities of the "angel" and the "monster" in the two primary female characters of her novel can be seen as a personal statement about the conflict between passion and passivity in her own life.

Author of ClassicNote and Sources

Teddy Wayne, author of ClassicNote. Completed on July 13, 2003, copyright held by GradeSaver.

Updated and revised Caitlin Vincent January 31, 2009. Copyright held by GradeSaver.

Brontë, Charlotte. Jane Eyre. London: Penguin Books, 1996.

Margarete Rubik and Elke Mettinger-Schartmann. A Breath of Fresh Eyre: Intertextual and Intermedial Reworkings of Jane Eyre. New York: Editions Rodopi B.V., 2007.

Elsie B. Michie. Charlotte Brontë's Jane Eyre: A Casebook. New York: Oxford University Press, 2006.

Jean Rhys. Wide Sargasso Sea. New York: Penguin Books, Ltd., 2001.

Jasper Fforde. The Eyre Affair: A Thursday Next Novel. New York: Penguin Books, Ltd., 2001.

Sue Thomas. Imperialism, Reform, and the Making of Englishness in Jane Eyre. New York: Palgrave Macmillan, 2008.

Lorna Ellis. Appearing to Diminish: Female Development and the British Bildungsroman, 1750-1850. Lewisburg: Bucknell University Press, 1999.

Karen Smith Kenyon. The Brontë Family: Passionate Literary Geniuses. Breckenridge: Twenty-First Century Books, 2002.

Sandra M. Gilbert and Susan Gubar. The Madwoman in the Attic: The Woman Writer and the Nineteenth-Century Literary Imagination. New Haven: Yale Nota Bene, 2000.

David Cody. "Charlotte Bronte: A Brief Biography." The Victorian Web. 2006-04-19. 2009-01-11. <http://www.victorianweb.org/authors/bronte/cbronte/brontbio.html>.

Jessica Menzo Russel Whitaker. "The Governess in Nineteenth-Century Literature: Introduction." Nineteenth-Century Literary Criticism on eNotes.com. 2006-01-01. 2009-01-14. <http://www.enotes.com/nineteenth-century-criticism/governess-nineteenth-century-literature>

Freeman, Janet H. "Speech and Silence in Jane Eyre" in Studies in English

Literature, 1500-1900, Vol. 24, No. 4, Nineteenth Century (Autumn 1984), pp. 683-700.

Solomon, Eric. "Jane Eyre: Fire and Water" in College English, Vol. 25, No. 3 (December 1963), pp. 215-217.

Kreilkamp, Ivan. "Unuttered: Withheld Speech and Female Authorship in 'Jane Eyre' and 'Villette'" in NOVEL: A Forum on Fiction, Vol. 32, No. 3, Victorian Fiction after New Historicism (Summer 1999), pp. 331-354.

Gilbert, Sandra M. "Plain Jane's Progress" in Signs, Vol. 2, No. 4 (Summer 1977), pp. 779-804.

Grudin, Peter. "Jane and the Other Mrs. Rochester: Excess and Restraint in 'Jane Eyre'" in NOVEL: A Forum on Fiction, Vol. 10, No. 2 (Winter 1977), pp. 145-157.

Essay: Women in Literature: Examining Oppression Versus Independence in Henry V and Jane Eyre

by Kathern Armstrong
December 06, 2002

"In many different societies, women, like colonised subjects, have been relegated to the position of 'Other,' 'colonised' by various forms of patriarchal domination. They thus share with colonised races and cultures an intimate experience of the politics of oppression and repression."

This statement is valid for Catherine from Henry V whereas Hostess

Quickly, Miss Temple and Jane are portrayed as more self-determining and independent than oppressed. Henry V takes place in medieval times, when women were thought of as nothing more than property and their only function was to produce offspring. Catherine, from Henry V is controlled by the male patriarchal figures in her life, like her father King Charles and King Henry and Hostess Quickly has no patriarchal figures, and is very outspoken and self-assured. Jane Eyre took place during the Victorian era, when women were still being treated like property; however, there were some women who had the ability to be independent. Miss Temple and Jane exemplify female independence.

Catherine, the princess of France in Henry V is oppressed by first her father and later King Henry. Her function in the play is to unite France and England by marrying Henry and producing an heir who would be both French and English. She is representative of the typical aristocratic female of the time. Her marriage is arranged by her father, not because he thinks Henry would be well suited for her, but for political reasons. He sent the French Ambassador to offer dukedoms and Catherine in marriage to Henry in exchange for his agreement to refrain from attacking France,

"...th'ambassador from the French comes back,/tells Harry that the King doth offer him/Catherine his daughter, and with her, to dowry,/Some petty and unprofitable dukedoms./ The offer likes not." (3.0. 27-31).

Henry does not accept these terms and wages war on France. Henry wins the war, and becomes King of France and he still wants to marry Catherine, even though she has never shown interest in him. Henry decides to consult Charles about the marriage, "shall Kate be my wife?" (5.2.312). Charles replied "so please you" (5.2.313), meaning that the decision is left up to Henry, as to whether he wants to marry Catherine, she is never consulted about the marriage. So Catherine must marry Henry. In a rather comical scene, Catherine asks her maid Alice to help her learn English, as she knows she must marry Henry, who is French. Thus Catherine must give up her culture and her way of life in France in order to marry Henry, and unfortunately she is never even asked about what she wants to do with her future.

Hostess Quickly, Miss Temple and Jane represent the complete opposite of Catherine. Where she is oppressed by patriarchal figures; they are independent women who shape their own destinies despite patriarchal figures from attempting to control them.

In Henry V, after the death of Falstaff, Bardolf and Pistol discuss the fact that in their opinion he will go to hell. Hostess Quickly never hesitated to join in with her opinion, she said "nay, sure he's not in hell. He's in Arthur's bosom. A made a finer end, and went away an it had been any christom child. A parted ev't just between twelve and one, ev'n at the turning o'th' tide-for after I saw him fumble with the sheets, and play with the flowers..." (2.3.9-14). She felt no hesitation at forming her own opinion even though it was contradictory to that of the men. Quickly also chose to marry Pistol instead of Nim, even though she had previously been betrothed to him, she made her own decision about her marriage, unlike Catherine.

Miss Temple from the novel Jane Eyre is the children's favorite teacher at Lowood School. Her function in the novel is to act as a matriarchal figure to Jane, as she had never had such a role model in her life; Mrs. Reed was cruel and hated Jane, and her own mother died when Jane was very young. Miss Temple is represented as a woman who is independent and is not afraid to express her opinions despite male authority. When the children's breakfast had been burnt, she organized a lunch of bread and cheese for them. Mr. Brockelhurst, the owner of the school is a miser and was upset to hear that Miss Temple had fed the children an extra meal. He said "...and there is another thing which surprised me; I find, in settling accounts with the housekeeper that a lunch, consisting of bread and cheese has twice been served out to the girls during the past fortnight. How is this? I looked over the regulations and I find no such meal as lunch mentioned. Who introduced this innovation? And by what authority?" (Bront 53). It was Miss Temple who had arranged the lunches, she replied "I must be responsible for the circumstance, sir, the breakfast was so ill prepared that the pupils could not possibly eat it; and I dared not allow them to remain fasting will dinner-time" (Bront, 53). Here, Miss Temple demonstrated her independence and her refusal to be repressed by Mr. Brockelhurst. Miss Temple is indeed an independent woman who speaks her mind and is not afraid to go against the stipulations of her male boss.

From an early age Jane is portrayed as rebellious and independent in the face of repression. Jane's function in the novel is to grow and mature because this bildungsroman novel. Jane is the main character and her story begins when she is a young child and progresses through Jane's adulthood. Mrs. Reed, Jane's aunt and unwilling guardian tried to control Jane when she was a child. She once called Jane a liar and Jane retaliated heartily, she said "speak I must: I had been trodden on severely, but how?...I gathered my energies and launched them in this blunt sentence-'I am not deceitful: if I were I should say I loved you; but I declare I do not love you: I dislike you the worst of anybody in the world" (Bront 29).

Jane's attitude remained with her through adulthood. When she was living at Thornfield Hall she demonstrated her independence, despite Mr. Rochester's attempts to control her. During one particular night after dinner, Mr. Rochester summoned Jane to keep him company. He insisted that she move her chair closer and converse with him since he had no one else to have an intelligent conversation with. At first Jane obeys only because Mr. Rochester is her boss and she is his paid employee, but after his constant pompous attitude, she retorted

"I don't think, sir, you have the right to command me, merely because you are older then I, or because you have seen more of the world than I have; you claim to superiority depends on the use you have made of your time and experience" (Bront 117).

Jane refused to take any kind of repression from Rochester. She further demonstrated her strength when she leaves Rochester because she refuses to become his mistress. She leaves Thornfield on her own accord with nothing more than her meager belongings. Jane's independence leads her to family, something she had wished for desperately. Her cousin St. John proposes to her, and Jane proves her headstrong ways again by refusing to marry him, even though a marriage would mean security, Jane could not let herself be dependent. Her inheritance, which was beyond her control, further solidified her self-determination. The money allowed Jane to truly have the freedom she always knew she possessed.

The only character who is repressed is Catherine, her future was decided for her by her father and even though she did not really want to marry Henry, she said nothing and obeyed her father. Hostess Quickly was in control of her own destiny and married who she wanted. Miss Temple remained self-assured while Mr. Brockelhurst reprimanded her and Jane demonstrated independence in every aspect of her life, from her childhood rebellion at Gateshead, to her career choice and marriage.

Works Cited

Bront, Charlotte. Jane Eyre. Wordsworth Editions Limited. Hertfordshire: 1999.

Shakespeare, William. Henry V. Oxford University Press. Oxford: 1982.

Essay: Jane Eyre: The Independent and Successful Woman Of the Nineteenth Century

by Rebecca Kivak
March 22, 2000

Imagine a girl growing up around the turn of the nineteenth century. An orphan, she has no family or friends, no wealth or position. Misunderstood and mistreated by the relatives she does have, she is sent away to a school where the cycle of cruelty continues. All alone in the world, she seems doomed to a life of failure. What's a girl to do? Does she stand passively by and accept her fate, as the common belief of the times would have it? Or does she stand up for her rights and fight for the life of success she deserves? If the girl is Charlotte Bronte's heroine Jane Eyre, she takes the latter route. Although this may have shocked readers of the time, Jane's actions would open the door for a new interpretation of women.

Jane Eyre showed that it was possible for a woman in the nineteenth century to achieve independence and success on her own, no matter what odds were against her. The following paper will examine the stereotype of women that Jane and her creator, Bronte, sought to disprove, explore the obstacles that Jane encounters in her struggle, and show how she is able to overcome them to attain the life she has always dreamed of having.

During the 1800's, the time period in which Jane Eyre was written and the setting of the novel, women were stereotyped as being "submissive, dependent, beautiful, but ignorant" (Harris 42). They were seen only as trophies, meant to cling to the arms of men, but never meant to develop a mind of their own or to venture out on their own. This stereotype proved difficult for women to be taken seriously. Dissatisfied with this interpretation of her sex, Bronte attempted to change it by creating a heroine who possessed the antithesis of these traits. Indeed, Jane may be a plain woman, but she is an intelligent one; she is also self-confident, strong-willed, and morally conscious (Harris 42). She not only trusts in her ability to make decisions, but also in her freedom to do so. Such traits will be necessary to guide her in her journey to self-fulfillment.

The first obstacle that Jane comes across is her own background. Usually, one can count on family or position to get ahead in life; Jane has neither. Since infancy, she has not only worn the label of orphan, but also that of lower-class: her mother had been disinherited from the family fortune upon marriage to Jane's father, a poor clergymen. Jane also faces discouragement in the not one, but two environments in which she is raised. At Gateshead, she is despised by her Aunt Reed and her cousins John, Eliza, and Georgiana. They never let her forget her lack of wealth or position, or their abundance of both. They see her as nothing more than a servant, and treat her as such (Eagleton 41). At Lowood school, Jane finds the ultimate "monument to the destruction of the most basic human unit, the family"(Blom 87). Stationed with other girls like herself, under the watchful and unforgiving eye of Rev. Brocklehurst, she is further made aware of all that she lacks. Perhaps the most important of these is love. Jane's cries for love are mistaken by both Aunt Reed and Rev. Brocklehurst as outbursts of evil.

A constant obstacle that appears throughout Jane's life is oppression. Women of the time often had to deal with oppression because of the stereotype imposed upon them; it is no different with Jane. Whenever she tries to speak up for herself and her needs, she is always met with some form of resistance. It starts with Aunt Reed and Rev. Brocklehurst, who interpret her as being willfully disobedient. It continues with St. John Rivers, who sees her as being selfish and unworthy of God. Even Edward Rochester, the love of her life, finds fault with Jane's need to express herself; it's the one thing that keeps her from being totally possessed by him. Ironically, it may have been Bronte's decision to tell the story in the first-person point of view that most accentuates the constancy of this obstacle in Jane's life. This technique allowed Bronte to tell her heroine's story with an intensity that drew the reader into Jane's thoughts, feelings, and passions, an openness which Jane has often been deprived of in her own life (McFadden-Gerber 3290).

The most prominent obstacle Jane faces is male power. The four men that Jane must contend with throughout the book are symbolic of the sources of male power over women. There is John Reed, Jane's tormentor at Gateshead, who represents physical force and patriarchal family. There is also Rev. Brocklehurst, Jane's tormentor at Lowood; he signifies the social structures of class, education, and religion. Rochester represents attraction, and St. John moral and spiritual authority (Mitchell 302). The former two try to take advantage of Jane's seeming defenselessness as a child; the latter two try to take advantage of her seeming defenselessness as a woman.

Jane is able to overcome her background chiefly by two means: distance and chance. In leaving for Lowood, she escapes Gateshead and all its disorder; in leaving for Thornfield, she escapes Lowood and its disorder. Jane's later return to Gateshead is a victory in that it not only shows how well she has succeeded on her own, without the Reeds, but it also reveals that as she once needed them, they now need her (Eagleton 39). As for her state of poverty, Jane triumphs over that merely by chance. It is while staying with St. John and his sisters at Whitcross that she is made aware of her relation to them, and the great inheritance from their uncle that they now all share. This is Jane's first step in attaining the wealth and family that has been denied her for so long.

The next obstacle to fall is oppression. Before Jane is sent away to Lowood, she tells Aunt Reed that it is she, not Jane, who is willfully disobedient: "People think you are a good woman, but you are bad, bad-hearted. You are deceitful!" It is with this statement that Jane first feels her soul begin to "expand, to exult, with the strangest sense of freedom, of triumph" she has ever felt (Bronte 30). It is this feeling which drives her in the confrontations she has with Rev. Brocklehurst, Rochester, and St. John concerning their hold over her, and it is one which she resolves never to lose. Armed with this feeling, Jane makes full use of her privileges as narrator. She freely comments on the "role of women in society and the greater constraint imposed upon them", and tells how she is able to overcome both (McFadden-Gerber 3290).

Jane's triumph over male power is her biggest one of all. Her first victory is in overcoming her tormentors. She surpasses John Reed by succeeding in the one area where she had been expected to fail: life. It is Jane, whom he had assumed of being powerless and frail, who ends up outliving him. Jane wins her struggle with Rev. Brocklehurst by refusing to live the rest of her life at Lowood under his orders. Her departure from Lowood is symbolic of leaving her old life behind for a new one.

Leaving Lowood also brings Jane to her hardest challenge. Throughout her life, Jane has always been looking for the one thing, more than wealth or position, that has always seemed to evade her - love. As an adult, she finds it in two men: Rochester and St. John. She realizes that although both men have different views of her and different reasons for wanting to marry her, they share the same motive: ultimately, to "destroy her selfhood" (Blom 99). Rochester's love for Jane is not only spiritual, but passionate. Although she feels the same way about him, she refuses to be his mistress. "It would not be wicked to love me," Rochester protests. Jane stands her ground: "It would be to obey you" (Bronte 301). On the other hand, St. John's love for her is "merely spiritual"; for Jane, this will not do. Her refusal of him for such a reason is considered shocking at a time when women were "imagined as merely inhabiting bodies meant to bear children and being, in other respects, tasteless and without appetite" (Oates 7). By rejecting both men, Jane puts her needs before anyone else's (Blom 100). After achieving independence by finding a family in the Riverses and wealth in her inheritance, Jane is now free to return to Rochester to complete her triumph. Following the fire at Thornfield, she finds him not as powerful as he once was; this works well for her, because she is more powerful than she once was. Rochester welcomes Jane back with open arms, realizing that he will never possess her the way he once wanted to, but that she, in fact, will end up possessing him. Their subsequent marriage not only ends the many conflicts involved, but also fulfills every woman's wish of achieving both independence and love (Mitchell 302).

Jane Eyre proved to the world of the 1800's that the idea of a woman beating the odds to become independent and successful on her own was not as far-fetched as it may have seemed. Jane goes against the expected type by "refusing subservience, disagreeing with her superiors, standing up for her rights, and venturing creative thoughts" (McFadden-Gerber 3290). With such determination, she is able to emerge victorious over all that has threatened to stand in her way. She is not only successful in terms of wealth and position, but more importantly, in terms of family and love. These two needs which have evaded Jane for so long are finally hers; adding to her victory is her ability to enjoy both without losing her hard-won independence. As Jane was a role model for women in the nineteenth century, she is also a role model for women today. Her legacy lives on in the belief that as long as there are hopes and dreams, nothing is impossible.

Works Cited

Blom, Margaret. Charlotte Bronte. Boston: Twayne Publishers, 1977.

Bronte, Charlotte. Jane Eyre. 1847. New York: Bantam Books, 1981.

Eagleton, Terry. " Jane Eyre: A Marxist Study." Modern Critical Interpretations: Charlotte Bronte's Jane Eyre. Ed. Harold Bloom. Philadelphia: Chelsea House Publishers, 1987: 29-46.

"Jane Eyre." Nineteenth-Century Literary Criticism. Vol. 3. Ed. Laurie Lanzen Harris. Detroit: Gale Research Company, 1982: 42-3.

McFadden-Gerber, Margaret. "Critical Evaluation." Masterplots. Rev. 2nd edition. Vol. 6. Ed. Frank N. Magill. Englewood Cliffs: Salem Press, 1996: 3290-4.

Mitchell, Sally. "Jane Eyre." Critical Survey of Long Fiction. Vol. 3. Ed. Frank N. Magill. Englewood Cliffs: Salem Press, 1983: 297-302.

Oates, Joyce Carol. Introduction. Jane Eyre. By Charlotte Bronte. New York: Bantam Books, 1987: 5-14.

Quiz 1

1. **What is the color of the room Jane is locked in at Gateshead?**
   A. Fuchsia
   B. Red
   C. Blue
   D. Green

2. **Who is the servant at Gateshead?**
   A. Bessie
   B. Mrs. Reed
   C. Georgiana
   D. Mrs. Fairfax

3. **How does John Reed die?**
   A. Murder
   B. Tuberculosis
   C. Suicide
   D. Old age

4. **Who suggests that Jane attend school?**
   A. Bessie
   B. Mrs. Reed
   C. Mr. Lloyd
   D. Jane

5. **Whose ghost does Jane believe she sees while at Gateshead?**
   A. Her uncle's
   B. Her father's
   C. Her mother's
   D. Her sister's

6. **What religious movement is Mr. Brocklehurst a part of?**
   A. Victorianism
   B. Buddhism
   C. Evangelicalism
   D. Stoicism

7. **What teacher takes Jane under her wing at Lowood?**
    A. Miss Scatcherd
    B. Mr. Brocklehurst
    C. Helen Burns
    D. Miss Temple

8. **What student befriends Jane at Lowood?**
    A. Helen Burns
    B. Miss Temple
    C. Mary Rivers
    D. Diana Rivers

9. **An outbreak of what disease spreads throughout Lowood?**
    A. Typhus
    B. Leprosy
    C. Pneumonia
    D. Chicken pox

10. **What does Mr. Brocklehurst do with the money meant for Lowood school?**
    A. Publish books
    B. Create a second school
    C. Indulge his own family
    D. Fund his political causes

11. **How does Jane meet Mr. Rochester?**
    A. He is in the barn
    B. He is reading to Adèle
    C. He is on horseback
    D. He is digging a ditch

12. **Who is Adèle's mother?**
    A. Céline Varens
    B. Mrs. Fairfax
    C. Miss Ingram
    D. Bertha Mason

13. **Who is Jane's rival for Mr. Rochester's affections?**
    A. Céline Varens
    B. Mrs. Fairfax
    C. Miss Ingram
    D. Bertha Mason

14. **What is Jane's position at Thornfield?**
    A. Governess
    B. Maid
    C. Cook
    D. Seamstress

15. **What is Grace Poole's ostensible position at Thornfield?**
    A. Governess
    B. Maid
    C. Cook
    D. Seamstress

16. **What is the real reason for Grace Poole's employment?**
    A. To guard Bertha Mason
    B. To kill any intruders
    C. To act as Rochester's mistress
    D. To brainwash Jane

17. **What disguise does Mr. Rochester put on at one point?**
    A. Fortune-teller
    B. Magician
    C. Musician
    D. Solicitor

18. **To whom does Mr. Rochester constantly attribute the demonic laughter from the third story?**
    A. Adèle
    B. Grace Poole
    C. Mrs. Fairfax
    D. Bertha Mason

19. **Why did Mr. Rochester marry Bertha Mason?**
   A. For her wealth
   B. For her beauty
   C. For her madness
   D. As a favor to her brother

20. **Whom does Mr. Rochester first tell Jane that he wants to marry?**
   A. Jane
   B. Mrs. Fairfax
   C. Miss Ingram
   D. Bertha Mason

21. **What did Mrs. Reed promise her dying husband?**
   A. To put Jane in a suitable orphanage
   B. To put Jane in the care of suitable foster parents
   C. To give Jane an equal share of their fortune
   D. To love Jane as one of her own children

22. **Where did Jane's uncle seek his fortune?**
   A. Berlin
   B. Madeira
   C. Barcelona
   D. Amsterdam

23. **What item of Jane's clothing does Bertha Mason rip one night?**
   A. Her stockings
   B. Her wedding-veil
   C. Her bonnet
   D. Her corset

24. **What two natural elements are important symbols in the novel?**
   A. Fire and water
   B. Earth and water
   C. Fire and ice
   D. Water and air

25. **What might Bertha Mason's imprisonment symbolize in Victorian England?**
    A. The treatment of the insane
    B. The status of wealthy women
    C. The status of women in marriage
    D. The treatment of beautiful women

Quiz 1 Answer Key

1. **(B)** Red
2. **(A)** Bessie
3. **(C)** Suicide
4. **(C)** Mr. Lloyd
5. **(A)** Her uncle's
6. **(C)** Evangelicalism
7. **(D)** Miss Temple
8. **(A)** Helen Burns
9. **(A)** Typhus
10. **(C)** Indulge his own family
11. **(C)** He is on horseback
12. **(A)** Céline Varens
13. **(C)** Miss Ingram
14. **(A)** Governess
15. **(D)** Seamstress
16. **(A)** To guard Bertha Mason
17. **(A)** Fortune-teller
18. **(B)** Grace Poole
19. **(A)** For her wealth
20. **(C)** Miss Ingram
21. **(D)** To love Jane as one of her own children
22. **(B)** Madeira
23. **(B)** Her wedding-veil
24. **(C)** Fire and ice
25. **(C)** The status of women in marriage

Quiz 2

1. **Where does Jane go after she leaves Thornfield?**
   A. London
   B. Lowood
   C. Gateshead
   D. Whitcross

2. **What is the name of the house St. John takes her into?**
   A. Whit's End
   B. Moor House
   C. Marsh House
   D. Marshmellow

3. **What does Jane do for food before she is taken in by St. John?**
   A. She begs
   B. She hunts
   C. She works
   D. She prostitutes herself

4. **What name does Jane give the Rivers siblings?**
   A. Jane Eyre
   B. June Eyre
   C. Jane Elliott
   D. June Elliott

5. **How does St. John discovers Jane's true name?**
   A. He sees it on a scrap of paper
   B. He finds her passport
   C. She tells him while drunk
   D. He looks through her belongings

6. **Who loves St. John, though he cannot return her affections?**
   A. Jane
   B. Mary
   C. Miss Oliver
   D. Diana

7. **What work does Jane receive at Whitcross?**
   A. She teaches at St. John's school
   B. She is a governess to Mary
   C. She cleans St. John's school
   D. She is a governess to Diana

8. **Who leaves Jane her fortune?**
   A. Mrs. Reed
   B. John Eyre
   C. Mr. Reed
   D. St. John

9. **What does Jane do with her fortune?**
   A. She invests it in the school
   B. She gives it to Lowood
   C. She divides it among the Reed children
   D. She divides it among the Rivers children

10. **What sense does Mr. Rochester lose in the fire at Thornfield?**
   A. Speech
   B. Hearing
   C. Sight
   D. Touch

11. **What pseudonym did Charlotte Brontë use while writing the novel?**
   A. George Orwell
   B. Alexander Graham Bell
   C. Currer Bell
   D. George Eliot

12. **The supernatural, mysterious events of Jane Eyre mark it as what kind of novel?**
   A. Gothic
   B. Bildungsroman
   C. Cyberpunk
   D. Modernist

13. **The coming-of-age plot and development of Jane Eyre mark it as what kind of novel?**
    A. Gothic
    B. Bildungsroman
    C. Cyberpunk
    D. Modernist

14. **In what year was Jane Eyre published?**
    A. 1737
    B. 1809
    C. 1847
    D. 1912

15. **What does Bertha Mason do in Mr. Rochester's bedroom?**
    A. Give Mr. Rochester a kiss
    B. Read a book
    C. Set fire to his bed
    D. Faint

16. **Which literary tradition does Charlotte Brontë invoke in her characterization of Mr. Rochester?**
    A. The oppressive male protagonist
    B. The knight in shining armor
    C. The wiser male friend
    D. The Byronic hero

17. **How many stages of Jane's development are in the novel?**
    A. Five
    B. Four
    C. Eight
    D. Three

18. **What are the names of Mr. Reed's three children?**
    A. John, Jane, and Mary
    B. John, Eliza, and Georgiana
    C. Patrick Branwell, Emily, and Jane
    D. Edward, Eliza, and Ann

19. **How old is Jane when the novel begins?**
    A. Five years old
    B. Eight years old
    C. Twelve years old
    D. Ten years old

20. **Which of the teachers at Lowood School has a special bond with Jane?**
    A. Miss Scratcherd
    B. Mr. Brocklehurst
    C. Miss Burns
    D. Miss Temple

21. **What is Mr. Rochester's full name?**
    A. Patrick Branwell Rochester
    B. John Edward Rochester
    C. Edward Mason Rochester
    D. Edward Fairfax Rochester

22. **What term is inscribed on Helen Burns' tombstone?**
    A. Quandam
    B. Regnat Populus
    C. Resurgam
    D. Pax

23. **Which character is particularly cruel to Helen Burns?**
    A. Jane Eyre
    B. Miss Scratcherd
    C. Miss Temple
    D. Mr. Rochester

24. **Who burns down Thornfield Manor?**
    A. Richard Mason
    B. Mrs. Fairfax
    C. Bertha Mason
    D. Mr. Rochester

25. **Why does Jane refuse to marry St. John?**

A. Because he does not love her
B. Because he is moving to India
C. Because he is a cruel man
D. Because he is too handsome

Quiz 2 Answer Key

1. **(D)** Whitcross
2. **(B)** Moor House
3. **(A)** She begs
4. **(C)** Jane Elliott
5. **(A)** He sees it on a scrap of paper
6. **(C)** Miss Oliver
7. **(A)** She teaches at St. John's school
8. **(B)** John Eyre
9. **(D)** She divides it among the Rivers children
10. **(C)** Sight
11. **(C)** Currer Bell
12. **(A)** Gothic
13. **(B)** Bildungsroman
14. **(C)** 1847
15. **(C)** Set fire to his bed
16. **(D)** The Byronic hero
17. **(A)** Five
18. **(B)** John, Eliza, and Georgiana
19. **(D)** Ten years old
20. **(D)** Miss Temple
21. **(D)** Edward Fairfax Rochester
22. **(C)** Resurgam
23. **(B)** Miss Scratcherd
24. **(C)** Bertha Mason
25. **(A)** Because he does not love her

Quiz 3

1. **What is Grace Pool's particular vice?**
   A. Eating sweets
   B. Allowing Bertha Mason to roam around the house
   C. Drinking gin
   D. Playing cards and gambling

2. **Which of Charlotte Brontë's sisters died of tuberculosis?**
   A. Ann and Julia
   B. Emily and Ann
   C. Elizabeth and Maria
   D. Eliza and Georgiana

3. **After which figure in Charlotte Brontë's own life is the character of John Reed modeled after?**
   A. Her uncle
   B. Her father
   C. Her husband
   D. Her brother

4. **Bertha Mason's attack of her brother is evocative of what gothic creature?**
   A. The changeling
   B. The Byronic hero
   C. The zombie
   D. The vampire

5. **Which 20th century novel is a "prequel" to Charlotte Brontë's novel?**
   A. Wide Sargasso Sea
   B. Before Thornfield
   C. Mr. Rochester and Miss Mason
   D. Becoming Jane

6. **What happens to Eliza Reed after her mother's death?**
   A. She becomes a governess
   B. She becomes an actress in London
   C. She joins a French convent
   D. She commits suicide

7. **What does Bessie name her daughter?**
   A. Georgiana
   B. Jane
   C. Beth
   D. Eliza

8. **How does Helen Burns react to the poor treatment of her at Lowood school?**
   A. She turns the other cheek
   B. She sets the school on fire
   C. She plots to remove Mr. Brocklehurst from power
   D. She commits suicide

9. **What body part does Mr. Rochester lose in the fire at Thornfield?**
   A. His leg
   B. His arm
   C. His hand
   D. His foot

10. **What is Bertha Mason's background?**
   A. Creole
   B. Spanish
   C. American
   D. French

11. **How many times does Bertha Mason escape in the novel?**
   A. Six
   B. Two
   C. Four
   D. Three

12. **What is the last line of Jane Eyre?**
   A. "My Edward and I, then are happy"
   B. "We entered the wood, and wended homeward"
   C. "Reader, I married him"
   D. "Amen; even so come, Lord Jesus"

13. **What book does Jane read while hiding behind the curtains at Gateshead?**
   A. Henry, Earl of Moreland
   B. History of British Birds
   C. Gulliver's Travels
   D. Pamela

14. **What does Miss Temple give the students at Lowood when the breakfast porridge is burnt?**
   A. Apples
   B. Fresh porridge
   C. Bread and cheese
   D. Cakes and tea

15. **What happens when Jane first meets Mr. Brocklehurst?**
   A. She is given an extra portion of porridge
   B. She faints
   C. She is ordered to cut off her hair
   D. She breaks her slate

16. **What does Mr. Brocklehurst accuse Jane of being?**
   A. A witch
   B. A heathen
   C. An insolent child
   D. A liar

17. **Whose letter clears Jane of any fault against her aunt?**
   A. Bessie's
   B. Mr. Lloyd's
   C. Mr. Brocklehurst's
   D. Miss Temple's

18. **Where does Jane's uncle live?**
   A. London
   B. Madeira
   C. Rome
   D. Paris

19. **Who is the housekeeper at Thornfield Manor?**
    A. Bessie
    B. Grace Pool
    C. Mrs. Fairfax
    D. Bertha Mason

20. **Who disapproves of Jane's marriage with Mr. Rochester because of the age and class differences between them?**
    A. Mrs. Reed
    B. Georgiana Reed
    C. Grace Pool
    D. Mrs. Fairfax

21. **What is the first element of the gothic that Jane encounters during her stay at Thornfield manor?**
    A. The moving table
    B. The rotten fruit
    C. The strange laugh
    D. The mysterious portrait

22. **Which of the following is NOT one of Jane's skills as a governess?**
    A. German
    B. Painting and drawing
    C. Music
    D. French

23. **How does Jane attain her position at Thornfield Manor?**
    A. Her uncle writes a letter to Mr. Rochester
    B. She becomes a member of a governess agency
    C. Miss Temple recommends her to Mr. Rochester
    D. She places an advertisement in the newspaper

24. **What is the name of Mr. Rochester's dog?**
    A. Samson
    B. Shep
    C. Pilot
    D. Rover

25. **What happens to Mr. Rochester when Jane first meets him?**

A. He falls off his horse

B. He breaks his arm

C. Pilot jumps on him

D. He knocks Jane over

Quiz 3 Answer Key

1. **(C)** Drinking gin
2. **(C)** Elizabeth and Maria
3. **(D)** Her brother
4. **(D)** The vampire
5. **(A)** Wide Sargasso Sea
6. **(C)** She joins a French convent
7. **(B)** Jane
8. **(A)** She turns the other cheek
9. **(C)** His hand
10. **(A)** Creole
11. **(C)** Four
12. **(D)** "Amen; even so come, Lord Jesus"
13. **(B)** History of British Birds
14. **(C)** Bread and cheese
15. **(D)** She breaks her slate
16. **(D)** A liar
17. **(B)** Mr. Lloyd's
18. **(B)** Madeira
19. **(C)** Mrs. Fairfax
20. **(D)** Mrs. Fairfax
21. **(C)** The strange laugh
22. **(A)** German
23. **(D)** She places an advertisement in the newspaper
24. **(C)** Pilot
25. **(A)** He falls off his horse

Quiz 4

1. **Why does Jane feel comfortable speaking her mind to Mr. Rochester?**
   A. Because he reminds her of her uncle
   B. Because he is handsome
   C. Because he is short
   D. Because he is not handsome

2. **What are Jane's initial conclusions about Mr. Rochester?**
   A. That he is very kind and encouraging
   B. That he is very changeful and abrupt
   C. That he is very handsome and appealing
   D. That he is very tortured and seductive

3. **What does Jane say when Mr. Rochester asks if she thinks him to be handsome?**
   A. "Yes, sir"
   B. "A little"
   C. "Many would think so, sir"
   D. "No, sir"

4. **Who writes to St. John about Jane's inheritence from her uncle?**
   A. Mrs. Reed
   B. Mr. Mason
   C. Mr. Briggs
   D. Mr. Rochester

5. **What does Miss Temple give to Jane and Helen during their tea together?**
   A. Cookies
   B. Seed cake
   C. Chocolate
   D. Fruit

6. **How does Mr. Brocklehurst punish the seeming "vanity" of one of his students?**
   A. He makes her stand on a stool for ten hours
   B. He starves her
   C. He forces her to cut off her hair
   D. He beats her

7. **Where does St. John want to take Jane as his missionary wife?**
   A. Madeira
   B. India
   C. Africa
   D. Greece

8. **What is the literary term used to describe this type of novel of development?**
   A. Romance novel
   B. Bildungsroman
   C. Fable
   D. Gothic novel

9. **What happens just as Jane is about to accept St. John's marriage proposal?**
   A. She has a hallucination about her future in India
   B. She faints
   C. She hears a thunderstorm approaching
   D. She hears Mr. Rochester calling her name

10. **What is the name of Mr. Rochester's second house?**
    A. Ferndean
    B. Marsh's End
    C. Moor House
    D. Thornfield Manor

11. **At what point in time does Jane narrate the plot of the novel?**
    A. One year after the events of the novel
    B. Ten years after the events of the novel
    C. Ten years before the events of the novel
    D. Five years after the events of the novel

12. **What happens to Jane and Mr. Rochester after their marriage?**
    A. They have a son
    B. They die in a house fire
    C. They write a novel about their romance
    D. They move to London

13. **What is Adèle's country of origin?**
    A. England
    B. Italy
    C. Greece
    D. France

14. **Who represents the literary tradition of the Madwoman in the Attic?**
    A. Jane Eyre
    B. Grace Poole
    C. Miss Ingram
    D. Bertha Mason

15. **What does Mr. Rochester want Jane to do after his marriage to Bertha Mason is revealed?**
    A. Become his second wife
    B. Continue to work as Adele's governess
    C. Leave Thornfield Manor forever
    D. Become his mistress

16. **What is the color of the room in which Mr. Reed died?**
    A. Red
    B. Blue
    C. Black
    D. Green

17. **How many years does Jane work as a teacher at Lowood School?**
    A. Two
    B. Five
    C. Eight
    D. Three

18. **What present does Mr. Rochester bring Adèle after one of his trips?**
    A. A dress
    B. A purse
    C. A puppy
    D. A bag of chocolates

19. **What does Jane do after she leaves Thornfield Manor and runs out of money?**
    A. She travels to London
    B. She begs for food
    C. She becomes a prostitute
    D. She writes for a newspaper

20. **What is the name of the servant at Moor House?**
    A. Bessie
    B. Georgiana
    C. Eliza
    D. Hannah

21. **What false name does Jane give herself while staying at Moor House?**
    A. Jane Rochester
    B. Jane Reed
    C. Jane Mason
    D. Jane Elliott

22. **How much money does Jane's uncle leave her upon his death?**
    A. 2,000 pounds
    B. 5,000 pounds
    C. 10,000 pounds
    D. 20,000 pounds

23. **How does Mrs. Reed die?**
    A. She has a stroke
    B. She overdoses on opium
    C. She drowns
    D. She commits suicide

24. **Where is Jane when Helen Burns dies?**
    A. Playing in the garden
    B. Waiting outside Helen's room
    C. Sleeping in Helen's bed
    D. Studying for her exams

25. **Which 19th-century poet was the inspiration for the concept of the Byronic hero?**
    A. Lord Grey de Byron
    B. John Byron Gordon
    C. Captain John Byron
    D. George Gordon Byron

Quiz 4 Answer Key

1. **(D)** Because he is not handsome
2. **(B)** That he is very changeful and abrupt
3. **(D)** "No, sir"
4. **(C)** Mr. Briggs
5. **(B)** Seed cake
6. **(C)** He forces her to cut off her hair
7. **(B)** India
8. **(B)** Bildungsroman
9. **(D)** She hears Mr. Rochester calling her name
10. **(A)** Ferndean
11. **(B)** Ten years after the events of the novel
12. **(A)** They have a son
13. **(D)** France
14. **(D)** Bertha Mason
15. **(D)** Become his mistress
16. **(A)** Red
17. **(A)** Two
18. **(A)** A dress
19. **(B)** She begs for food
20. **(D)** Hannah
21. **(D)** Jane Elliott
22. **(D)** 20,000 pounds
23. **(A)** She has a stroke
24. **(C)** Sleeping in Helen's bed
25. **(D)** George Gordon Byron